24 tales

MORE APPALACHIAN GHOST STORIES, LEGENDS & MYSTERIES

EDITED BY
TERRY SHAW

HOWLING HILLS PUBLISHING

Howling Hills is a publisher of nonfiction books from Greater Appalachia, an area we loosely define as North Georgia to Maine.
Learn more at *howlinghillspublishing.com*.

BOOK DESIGN
Travis Akard

COVER PHOTOGRAPHS
©Spencer Selover, ©Lucas Pezeta, ©Frank Cone, ©James Sutton

24 Tales: More Appalachian Ghost Stories, Legends & Mysteries
©2024 Howling Hills Publishing

First published in the United States of America in 2024
by Howling Hills Publishing, Kingsport, Tennessee.

Howling Hills Publishing, LLC
Kingsport, Tennessee
www.howlinghillspublishing.com

All rights reserved. No part of this book may be reproduced in any form without written permission from the copyright owners.

All images in this book have been reproduced with the consent of the artists concerned, and every effort has been made to ensure accurate credits. We apologize if there are any inaccuracies that may have occurred and will resolve inaccurate or missing information in subsequent reprintings of this book and/or at *howlinghillspublishing.com*.

ISBN: 979-8-9881621-3-1
CIP data is available through the Library of Congress.

24 tales

**MORE APPALACHIAN GHOST STORIES,
LEGENDS & MYSTERIES**

Ghost Skeptics Can Change More Than You Think

I used to work at a haunted newspaper, though we rarely talked about it. Some employees believed The Corry Journal had ghosts, and others thought we were crazy, so what was there to say? The evidence was fleeting.

Voices.

Footsteps.

Lights that turned on and off at the oddest times.

This could be unnerving, especially if you were alone late at night in that creaky old building. But in 1986, The Journal was run by legendary newspaperman George R. Sample Jr., who was blunt, no nonsense, and dismissed all talk of ghosts.

The publisher of my hometown newspaper was a serious man.

Sample had hitchhiked from Penn State to the northwestern corner of the commonwealth during a snowstorm to interview for a reporter's job back in 1946. He worked at *The Journal* until his death in 2008. During that time, he'd been nominated for a Pulitzer Prize for editorial writing, served as vice chairman of the board for a major newspaper chain, then started his own news empire, now run by his son. He was my friend, mentor, and as hard-headed as they come.

"Of course he doesn't want to admit the place has ghosts," a reporter named Mike Hudson once told me. "Who do you think they're here to haunt?"

Hudson had a point.

I hadn't thought much about *The Journal*'s spirits until last year, when Howling Hills published *23 Tales: Appalachian Ghost Stories, Legends & Other Mysteries*. I wanted to write a story about the newspaper for the anthology, but many of my coworkers had passed, and I didn't feel comfortable relying solely on my own memory. Truth be told, the idea seemed a little silly.

I did manage to reach Andrew Sproveri, who spent thirteen years at the place, first running the prepress camera, then eventually becoming head pressman.

"Here's an odd question out of the blue after almost forty years," I said to him. "Is *The Journal* haunted?"

Sproveri's response was immediate and emphatic.

"It is absolutely, 100 percent haunted," he insisted.

"That building is the creepiest place to be alone," he added. "Your imagination can get away from you. But I saw apparitions of some type at least a half-dozen times. I would be in the camera room and would turn around and see a foggy figure in the corner of the ceiling."

Or he would be walking in the pressroom and hear a loud clatter and bang as big wrenches fell off the wall, almost as if someone were knocking things down behind him.

After talking to Andy, I felt a *little* less crazy. Yet the anthology deadline passed before I reached anyone else.

I tried again with the publication of *24 Tales: More Appalachian Ghost Stories, Legends & Mysteries*. This time I wanted to talk to a ghost skeptic, maybe for George's sake, and knew just the person. In fact, I've known Bob Williams since I was ten years old and he was eight. Williams, who recently retired after thrity-four years at *The Journal*, had been general manager, then succeeded Sample as publisher.

Expecting to be mocked, I asked him if *The Journal* was haunted. Though Williams used more colorful language than Sproveri, he gave a similar answer. Then my friend and I laughed like we were still in grade school.

"I would always see things out of the corner of my eye," he said "Or feel extremely cold spots in the basement."

Often when alone in his office, Bob's coffee cup would disappear, only to be found in another room he hadn't been in that morning. Once he turned off every downstairs light, but before going upstairs, noticed the farthest light had been turned back on.

"It was like someone was pulling pranks on me," he said.

One time he was alone upstairs, heard a crazy racket in the pressroom, then went downstairs to find the place completely dark. He went back to his office. It happened again, only then every light was on.

"That's when I went home for the night," he said.

I believed him.

"But George never bought into any of this, did he?" I asked.

"No," Williams answered. "But he said I wasn't the first person to mention it."

That slight acknowledgement surprised me.

The last time I saw George was on a visit to Corry in 2007. Both Mike Hudson and I had books out and our former boss had been delighted. Then eighty-three, he'd suffered multiple strokes, walked with a cane, and slowly shuffled into the newsroom with a limp and a drag of one foot. I'd known him most of my life, and it was heartbreaking. Yet as long as he could breathe, nothing could keep him from his beloved newspaper.

"Terry, if you find a job you love you'll never work a day in your life," he always told me.

I'd like to think he would be proud of Howling Hills Publishing, though he would probably call bull on a book of ghost stories. That's all right. Some of our contributors had their own skepticism. Consider **Steven Pappas** and an apparition that appears on his property.

"To be clear—and honest—I have never seen Jim Mitchell," Pappas wrote. "I know people who have put eyes on him—and they most definitely should not have: He's been dead a long time now. I have seen things that could be related to Jim Mitchell that I cannot explain. Logic has been lost, along with physics' unwavering laws. That's saying something because I'm pretty cynical. I am a journalist, with years behind me. I trust facts and science.

"The idea of Jim Mitchell is cool to me. I suppose I want to believe in ghosts, UFOs, even Sasquatch, but facts—and the concrete, hard reality that comes with them—usually deprive me of such daydreams. Yet I cannot explain what happens on my family's property in rural Vermont, in my corner of a quiet, little town."

This year's anthology has twenty-four tales from twenty-four writers. **Jerry Sword** starts things off with a chilling tale of living in a haunted house, followed by **Suzy Trotta's** funny and frightening experiences visiting one owned by her parents. **Anna Wooliver Phillips**, **Jessica Fischer**, and **Brad Lifford** also write about haunted houses. While **Eleanor Scott** talks about her charming house, I would describe her quirky story as more of a mystery.

Again, family tales are a key part of this year's anthology. **Patty Ireland**, **Danita Dodson**, **Megan McKamey**, **Matt Hopkins**, and **Larry Thacker** tell stories from previous generations. **Sheri McCarter**, **Chrissie Anderson Peters**, **Victoria Jordan** and **Sue Dunlap** combine family history and personal experience. I report on a haunted marriage.

We have our share of Appalachian history: **Thom Tracy** on a mine tragedy from 1869 in Plymouth Township, Pennsylvania; **Jennie Ivey** on a heartbreaking disappearance in the Great Smoky Mountains National Park; and **Laura Still** on the Knoxville hotel where country legend Hank Williams spent his final night. **Doug Brown** mixes history and personal experience.

Other writers visited haunted locales: **Regina Zeyzus** a brewery in Erie, Pennsylvania, and **Raina Wiseman** a nail salon in Western North Carolina. Bad boy **Kevin Saylor** did hard time (for most of a night), in Tennessee's notorious Brushy Mountain prison. He started as a skeptic, but minds and situations can change.

Remember *The Corry Journal*? After 2008, a new twist was added to the story. Often in the early morning hours, then-Publisher Bob Williams would hear footsteps he recognized on the stairs.

A limp and a dragging foot.

A limp and a dragging foot.

A limp and a dragging foot

He's sure they belonged to our late mentor.

Whether you believe in ghosts, or are a skeptic like George Sample (who may now be a ghost himself), I hope you enjoy *24 Tales*!

TERRY SHAW
Howling Hills Publishing
September 2024

Contents

14	**A Haunting in Corn Valley**	Jerry Sword
19	**Bad Ghost**	Suzy Trotta
27	**The Outcasting**	Patty Ireland
38	**Friend Ghost**	Eleanor Scott
42	**The Girl at Union Station**	Regina Zeyzus
47	**Dread, Beauty, and Tragedy Come in Pink**	Brad Lifford
55	**A Promise that Haunts Through the Ages**	Thom Tracy
60	**The Bloody Seventh**	Danita Dodson
66	**Where's Dennis?**	Jennie Ivey
73	**I Carried the Sight**	Sue Weaver Dunlap
78	**Brushy Mountain Prison Blues**	Kevin Saylor
86	**An Easy Way to Get Rid of Ghosts**	Terry Shaw

Contents

91	**Stalking Old Moses Wharton**	Doug Brown
98	**The Knocking Spirit**	Megan McKamey
103	**Seventh Son**	Matt Hopkins
110	**Eddie's Apparition**	Sheri McCarter
116	**Long Gone Lonesome Blues**	Laura Still
123	**A Haunted Homeplace**	Jessica Fischer
129	**Belkis Salon and Spa and Spirits**	Raina Wiseman
133	**The Swinging Gate of Fern Lake Hollow**	Larry D. Thacker
143	**What Annie Saw**	Chrissie Anderson Peters
150	**The House on Bluebird Drive**	Anna Wooliver Phillips
155	**May All Your Dreams Come True**	Victoria Jordan
162	**I've Never Seen Jim Mitchell**	Steven Pappas

— ONE —

A Haunting in Corn Valley
Russell County, Virginia

JERRY SWORD

In the summer of 1991, I turned seventeen. I had grown up on a farm in Corn Valley, a rural part of Russell County, Virginia. When I say "rural" I really mean the middle of nowhere. Before I was old enough to drive, if I was lucky, I might have seen town limits twice a month during summer breaks from school.

My father had passed the year before, leaving only my mother and myself in a house that was built in the early 1920s. It needed quite a bit of work. Old rusted sheets of tin were stretched across a decaying roof, and when it rained, the echoes of water hitting the roof seemed to drift down the walls, and scatter into the darkest corners of the house. Buckets placed under leaks sat on floors weakened by time, almost ready to fall though.

My mother was in the early stages of crippling arthritis. At the time I was aware of her diagnosis, but my seventeen-year-old mind really did not grasp the severity of her condition. So there we were, a middle-aged woman in failing health and a teenage boy, alone on sixty acres of mountain farmland, desolation defined. The wide-open fields between us and a neighboring farm were vast and seemed to stretch to the horizon.

I always had a healthy fear of that old house. My father moved us there from Florida when I turned six, and I remember things from my childhood that had no real explanation. Seeing sudden movements out of the corner of my eye. Having items disappear from where they'd been left, only to turn up later in a different part of the house. Or worse, turning up exactly where you'd already looked for them. At times a sense of dread hung over the entire property.

As I grew older and my interests turned to girls and working a part-time job after school, my fear of the house seemed to subside. I would arrive home late at night, check in on my declining mother, and climb the steps to the second floor to sleep for a few hours before getting up to do it all over again.

I don't remember when the noises started. At first they were very subtle: floorboards creaking in the dead hours of the night and early morning. My mother was dealing with far more than failing health. She was learning to live without my father, her husband of thirty years. So it wasn't farfetched to hear these sounds and think she was restless, moving around at night.

The second floor layout was simple: two bedrooms across a hallway from each other. One was mine. I had taken it a few years before, after my sister moved out. The other room was empty except for a couple of beds. It was only used if my brother Robert happened to be home on leave from the Marine Corps, which didn't happen often. I remember the antique iron bed where he would sleep on those visits very vividly. It had probably been there since the house was built. I also remember how cold the room always was, even during the hottest days of summer. This was odd because we did not have the luxury of HVAC. Summers burned in that house, and all over that farm. But that room always remained cold to me, and I avoided it at all costs.

As the weeks and months crept by, the noises became louder and louder. I was hearing my mother's footsteps right outside my bedroom door at all hours of the night. She was walking into the room across the hall for some reason. To mask the late-night sounds, I began to leave my stereo on at night, with a CD on repeat until my alarm went off in the morning.

On one of those nights, I simply had enough. At around 4 a.m. I was awakened by the loud footsteps outside my door. I got out of bed, agitated and ready to tell my mother she needed to stop doing this every night. I opened the door to confront her and peered into darkness.

No one was there.

It felt as if I had stepped into a void. The house was quiet, except for the sound of my mom softly breathing in the bedroom downstairs. The racket had ceased the instant I threw the door open, and heat permeated the house.

I closed the door and at some point decided I was losing my mind. I climbed back into my bed but never closed my eyes, frightened by what occurred and waiting for daylight.

When the light finally came, I asked my mother why she had been walking around the house so late at night, hoping she would provide an explanation. The only assurance I got was that she was no longer capable of climbing the stairs; when night came, she was always in bed. This shook me to the core.

I moved out permanently a year later, after the farm was sold. For that entire year I slept on a couch in my mother's bedroom downstairs. I never told anyone about it. For the longest time, I dismissed it all as the result of an overactive imagination. My mom moved closer to town, closer to medical care and other family members who would help look after her. I moved into the arms of the woman who would become my wife, and began a new chapter. Whatever I had experienced back on that farm, I chose to leave it behind me.

Almost a decade later I found myself at my brother Robert's home in South Florida. I was there with my wife and my young son on vacation. One late night my brother and I were talking in the kitchen after everyone else had gone to bed. The conversation turned to the old farm and all the fear

I had tried to forget.

"Did you ever have anything strange happen to you in that old house?" he asked.

Even the question terrified me.

He went on to tell me of a full-bodied apparition he encountered as a teenager. My father witnessed the same apparition the same night.

One story that intertwined with my own was of a night he went to bed in that cold room across the hall. Something unseen sat down on the edge of the old iron bed and began ripping the blankets from his body. He was so terrified he could not even scream. Whatever Robert was talking about was the same thing I heard walking the halls late at night. It was why I slept on the couch for the last year I lived there. This would be our first of many conversations about the old farm in Corn Valley.

Today the house is abandoned and sinking into the earth. Countless stories could be told about the place, but my brother and I agree on one thing above all else. Neither of us would spend a night there again. Not for any amount of money.

JERRY SWORD *is a storyteller who grew up in Russell County, Virginia and now lives in Bristol. He composed the song "Dead Man's Hands" for the American World Pictures movie "Grizzly Park." He has also written and directed the documentaries "This Place is Haunted" (2013) and "Season of the Witch" (2022). He's at work on the documentary "Under Broken Sky."*

— TWO —

BAD GHOST
Rutherford County, Tennessee

SUZY TROTTA

After I moved out and went to college, my parents renovated a farmhouse in Rutherford County, Tennessee, next door to my uncle's house. This was great for my dad; he could now drive the one-eighth of a mile each morning to his brother's house to drink coffee and talk loudly at 5 a.m. This was not great for me because that farmhouse had something very bad in it.

When they first bought the house, they renovated almost everything before moving in. It was a 1940s rancher and had been the main house of the farm that would soon be a subdivision thanks to my uncle. It wasn't that spectacular, but the wood floors were pretty, and the period-perfect bathrooms made my heart sing. I do love a nice pink or green tub with matching tile. My parents left these intact, which I thought was cool.

This was the early 1990s and copper theft was at an all-time high, so when they replaced the kitchen plumbing, they asked my boyfriend at the time if he would spend the night in the house to make sure no one broke in and stripped the copper. In retrospect, I don't know what that skinny modern dancer would have done to a potential thief except scream loud SAT words at him, but he agreed.

Jon camped out in the back den and called me the next day to give me the rundown on his sleepover.

"Who was the dude stomping around the living room just before dawn?" he asked.

"Didn't you get up to check?"

He had, after all, been tasked with guarding the house.

"I did, but by the time I got up, there wasn't anybody there. I thought maybe it was your dad."

There was no love lost between Jon and my dad. (*What do you see in that little wimp?* my father asked me more than once.) So if he had thought it was my dad, he might have avoided him.

I asked my dad about it.

"There wasn't nobody in there because we just refinished those damn floors. I told Jon not to walk in there. He didn't walk in there, did he?" To my dad, this would be just the kind of dumb thing Jon would do.

A quick check of the living room floor proved that no one had disturbed the new finish, which was good, but also perplexing. If no one had disturbed the finish, how had someone in heavy boots walked all over it?

I stood with my father just outside that living room later that day, looking at the newly shining floors. My father was uncharacteristically quiet and thoughtful as he stared. My mother walked by and said, "It's probably just that Civil War soldier."

This is not as loony as it sounds. I had, after all, grown up in a haunted house. A happily haunted house, but one we all agreed had some kind of presence in it we could not fully understand or communicate with. It was just a fact of life, like the yellow dog that howled outside my parents' bedroom window at night, or the fat possum that came and ate the outdoor cat food. We had all seen these things, but there wasn't a lot of reason to talk about them. Except when the possum got so fat he had trouble waddling up and down the patio steps to get the cat food or when my father, in a fit of pique, fired off his "squirrel gun" at what he called "Yella Dawg" at 2 a.m. one sleepless night.

The entity in that house had never done anything as exciting as those creatures of the night.

Unlike my childhood home, I only stayed in this remodeled farmhouse for holidays or the occasional weekend. A lot of things had changed in our family. I wouldn't have said it at the time, but there were plenty of places I would rather be, and that farmhouse was never somewhere I called home.

Being a lifelong insomniac, I usually stayed up reading until 2 or 3 a.m. before falling asleep. When I stayed in that house, I would shut my bedroom door, because my father snored like a freight train and my mother ground her teeth like a creature from hell. Neither were conducive to relaxation.

I had long ago forgotten about the mysterious footsteps and my mother's Civil War soldier comment as I lay in bed one night, reading and most likely making my way through a bag of chips.

I yelped and came out of the bed when someone pounded on my door, shaking it in its frame and making my bed shake as well.

"Who's there?" I squawked, which sounded dumb to my ears even as it left my lips. There were only three people in the house. Who could it be but my mother or father? And why wouldn't they just open the door? Because this was a house where my father not only saw fit to do his "business" with the door open, he also hung a mirror in the hall, allowing him to watch the news or *Wheel of Fortune* while he did that business. He also occasionally asked me to bring him a cup of coffee while he watched TV while he did his business. In other words, we had few physical boundaries in our family.

"Hello?" I figured it was worth asking one more time before I got out of that high, antique bed, which—now that I thought about it—had a lot of room for someone to hide underneath, my mother's double bed skirts cloaking any person or creature who chose to lie in wait.

With still no answer, I gingerly put my feet on the floor, now fully paranoid and mindful of anything or anyone wanting to grab my ankles and tiptoed to the door. I cracked it open, unsure of what I was so afraid of. Peeking through the crack, I saw... nothing. No one was there. I flung the door open all the way.

Nothing.

I could hear my father snoring and my mother grinding her teeth all the way down the hallway. My heart pounding, I sneaked down to their room to confirm with my own eyes that they were still in bed, and there they were, sound asleep.

I ran back to my room and huddled in bed, scared to death. Reading was now out of the question, as was sleeping, or getting up to go to the bathroom. I stayed awake, pumped with adrenaline, until the sun lightened the horizon and I finally felt safe enough to close my eyes.

The next day, I asked my parents if they had been up in the night, but when they said they hadn't, I didn't push the issue. Yes, I had been scared, but maybe there was another explanation for what had happened. Unlike my childhood home, there didn't seem to be any mutual understanding—despite my mother's comment about the soldier—that anything out of the ordinary was happening in this house.

The next time I stayed there, I came prepared. I checked under the bed before getting in with my snacks and books, and kept the door open, making sure no one could pound on it without me seeing them. I must have fallen asleep reading, because I suddenly had the oddest sensation of being half awake and terrified. I knew I was in the bed and the lamp was still on, but I couldn't open my eyes and try as I might, I could not scream. All I wanted to do was scream. It felt like something had me pinned down there, unwilling to let me go. I was in my body and outside my body at the same time.

When I finally scrambled up to the surface of full consciousness, I sat up, looking around, my pulse throbbing my whole body, trying to figure out what just happened. With no explanation, I did what I would do so often in that house: Waited for the sun to come up so I could go to sleep.

I would go on to have a few more of these night terror/sleep paralysis type of events in that house. I have never had them anywhere else or since. They are something I associate only with whatever was sharing space with us there.

The next Christmas, my oldest brother and his family came to stay. My brother and his wife slept in the guest bedroom next to mine. It was their first overnight visit in the house, and while I slept peacefully, the house's "mojo" had apparently found new victims to wreak havoc on.

My big-ass brother, a twenty-year Navy veteran, asked me with a shaking voice the next day if I had ever noticed anything strange in the house.

"Like what?" I asked, hedging, not wanting to sound crazy if he wasn't talking about what I thought he was talking about.

"Like a damn ghost," my sister in-law, blunt as ever, interjected. I told them about the pounding experience, and they told me about their sleepless night.

As they lay in bed trying to go to sleep, the room temperature quickly dropped. Just as they both remarked about this to each other, they smelled a very floral perfume, first faint, and then overwhelming. Just as they were about to ask each other about that, they heard music. And then everything stopped. As I had, they didn't fall asleep until the sky started to lighten.

"I thought maybe it was Grandma," my brother said, referring to our father's mother, who had died in my uncle's house next door.

I quickly set him straight on this. "If Grandma was going to haunt us, it would be to yell, 'Reagan is a damn son of a bitch!' and then fry bologna in the kitchen. Plus, she never wore perfume."

He seemed to think this was reasonable and proceeded to never visit the farmhouse again.

I only stayed in that house once by myself, but it was enough. Knowing I wouldn't be able to sleep in any of the bedrooms, I set up camp on the couch in the living room, fortifying myself by turning on the TV and all the lights. Every time I closed my eyes, I heard noises from the hallway to the bedrooms. Small noises, possibly old house noises, probably nothing noises. But noises. It wasn't so much what I was hearing, though, as what I was feeling: something really did not want me to be in that house and the feeling was mutual.

My father later told me he wasn't comfortable being alone there either. Once when my mother was out of town, he—a 6'4" man who had won his share of ass whoopins—said he couldn't stop imagining someone coming up from behind him to choke him to death. He wouldn't sit anywhere in the house where someone could get behind him. This was a man who had a handgun in probably every end table, and he was terrified. He knew it was irrational, but the thoughts wouldn't stop. I didn't think he was crazy. I knew exactly what he meant.

I guess whatever was in that house didn't affect my parents as much as it did me and my brother, because they stayed there a long time. I did my best to stay far away from what I felt there. I wouldn't feel it again until years later in a home I listed as a real estate agent, but I would instantly recognize it for what I now knew it was: a very bad ghost.

SUZY TROTTA *is the author of* Open House: Mostly True Tales of Crazy in Southern Real Estate. *She has also had work in The Knoxville Writers Guild* ReView. *You can read about another one of her ghost encounters in* 23 Tales: Appalachian Ghost Stories, Legends & Other Mysteries. *Suzy lives in Knoxville, Tennessee, with her husband, cats, and baby angel dog, Jolene.*

— THREE —

THE OUTCASTING
Six Mile, Tennessee

PATTY IRELAND

When I was twelve, a ninety-three-year-old family member told me a story I have never forgotten. As we sat on her porch drinking Kool-Aid and watching the sun descend behind the mountains, I asked if she had ever seen a ghost. She explained that, in fact, she had. Of all places, it happened in a church back in 1921. This is the story as it was told to me.

It was right in the middle of Prophet Hobart's Sunday morning message—the part where he spoke in tongues and then gave the discernment—when old Brother Martin stood up all a sudden, resting his trembling hands on the pew in front of him.

"Churches can't be haunted," he interrupted loudly, his thick, gray eyebrows rising to reveal deeply furrowed lines in his forehead. "Can't be," he repeated. "Haints won't come anywhere near a church house."

Prophet Hobart stopped and glared down at Brother Martin from his lofty perch behind the hundred-year-old pulpit. "Well, this one is surely haunted, friend, and if we don't cast out that spirit, we'll all be sorry."

"Hog wash," Brother Martin declared.

Prophet Hobart narrowed his eyes. "Now look here, Martin. Scripture says that even Jesus came face to face with unclean spirits in the house of the Lord."

Brother Martin shook his head. "Never heard of such. If it's true, then just whereabouts in the good book does it say that?" he asked.

"Right here." Prophet Hobart picked up his large, leather-bound Bible, holding it high in the air.

Then he slammed the old book down on the lectern and eagerly turned to Mark 1:21-28: "And they went into Cappernaum and immediately on the Sabbath He entered the synagogue and was teaching. And there was in that synagogue a man with an unclean spirit. And he—that's the demon spirit they're referring to now that took over that man—cried out, 'What have you to do with me, Jesus of Nazareth? Have you come to destroy me? I know who you are—the Holy One of God.' But Jesus rebuked him, saying 'Be silent, and come out of him!'

"Here's the truth, Martin: If we don't hold a proper outcasting, then the ghostly spirit that chose this church as its resting spot will find somebody to get into and make a shell out of his soul."

That was how talk of the outcasting at the Piney Grove Primitive Baptist Church in Six Mile, Tennessee, first began. I was eleven going on twelve, observing from the second-to-last pew, squeezed between my mother on one side and my Great Aunt Grace on the other. None of us had ever seen the prophet questioned, much less challenged openly in the very midst of his sermon, about any subject. He was a prophet, after all, not just a preacher. He could foretell the future, speak the heavenly tongues of God and angels, interpret his own speaking, and discern both good and evil spirits.

"I will now continue, the good Lord willing," the prophet declared. "The Word says that in latter days some will depart from the faith by devoting themselves to deceitful spirits and demons. Not only that, but Matthew chapter twelve says when one of those unclean spirits—what most around here call a haint—is too confounded to descend straight to hell, then it lingers down here looking for a waterless place. This, friends, is a waterless place. There's no well, no creek, no river nearby. Nobody has been able to douse for water here for two hundred years or more. And Matthew says the spirit will stick fast to that waterless place once it locks onto a particular house. That house is this one, friends, the very house of the Lord, and the haint that's locked onto it is Sarah Nell Dunlap."

Miss Addie Thompson and Miss Catacomb Reed, two elderly spinsters who always sat together near the altar and knew Sarah Nell in their younger days, gasped out loud. Mother looked at Great Aunt Grace with fear in her eyes. Adults all over the church sat bolt upright in their hard wooden pews. Children who, minutes before, had been idly tinkering with their church dolls or drawing stick figures on scrap paper stopped and looked up.

All was silent.

My friend, Lottie Simpson, turned to me from the pew ahead. "I seen her once," she whispered. "I seen the ghost of Sarah Nell one night walking down this very church aisle."

Mrs. Simpson poked an elbow into Lottie's shoulder. "Shhhhh!"

I didn't tell, but I had seen her too. It happened one evening near twilight time after the Wednesday night Bible study. Daddy stayed home with Mother, whose time had come to give birth to my baby brother, Vern. Great Aunt Grace, who brought me to the church house, was out on the front lawn talking to other ladies. Me, Lottie, Ben Hufstedler and Joe-Mike Henson had been playing Kick the Wickey in the yard out back. It was Lottie's turn to kick the foot-long stick we'd found in the woods when I remembered that I left my church doll back inside on the pew.

"Don't kick yet, Lottie," I begged. "I want to see you kick farther than Ben with my own eyes. I'll be right back."

It seemed odd to go into the sanctuary when no one was there. It seemed kind of wrong somehow, as if I was intruding on the private space of the Holy Ghost himself by marching into his sacred quarters with dirt on my boots and my hair bow falling loose. But I needed my doll, so I pushed the heavy double doors open and moved forward in the semi-darkness toward "our" pew.

There was my doll, the one I named Beatrice, propped up on a hymnal. I grabbed her and started to run out when it occurred to me that this was my chance to play a few notes on the piano, something I'd always aimed to do. Stuffing Beatrice under one arm, I made my way up to the front, past the altar with its bouquet of daisies, faded now from the Sunday service, and over to the old upright. I laid Beatrice down and began picking out a few notes to the tune of "Where We'll Never Grow Old." That's when I thought I heard someone speak.

"Elmer?" the female voice said. "Are you here?"

Startled, I froze, my hands motionless over the ivories. I glanced out into the sanctuary but saw no one, picked up Beatrice and stood from the piano bench to make my way out of the sanctuary. That's when I saw her: beautiful, pale, translucent.

"Elmer? I'm waiting. I've been a waiting here a long time. Are you here?"

The young woman coming down the aisle in a homemade bridal gown looked past me, as if I did not exist. Then she turned her head left and right. I could see her dark hair done up in a bun on the top of her head as tiny wisps of curls fell from either side of her porcelain face. A silky veil flowed around her, enveloping her form in its pure whiteness as she floated like a cloud down the aisle ever closer to me.

Then she looked directly at me. I could not see her eyes clearly in the half-dark of twilight, especially as they were hidden by her veil, but I could tell her eyes were strange, as if they operated independently of a mind and soul. "You seen my Elmer?" she asked.

My eyes widened. "No ma'am. I haven't seen anybody by the name of Elmer."

"Don't you know him, child?" she questioned, tilting her lovely head to one side as she considered me. "Everybody knows my Elmer. I can't imagine that you don't know him too."

I swallowed hard. "No. I don't know anyone named Elmer. I don't think there's anybody here by that name."

She lifted both shoulders playfully, tilted back her head and laughed a tinkling laugh. "Course there is. Elmer is the most handsome bachelor 'round this town, child. All the girls are in love with him, but I'm his one true promised, his one and only betrothed."

I moved a step or two. "Well, miss, I got to go, really I do," I stuttered, clasping on to Beatrice and edging toward the aisle. "I hope you find him."

Just then she raised her slender arms, and with her graceful, white hands lifted the veil. That was when I could see that she had no eyes, only empty sockets of blackness.

I screamed a blood-curdling cry, shut both eyes tightly and placed my hands over them, as if doing so would somehow make her go away. I wrapped my body in my own arms, dropping Beatrice in the process. I slumped to the floor and rocked back and forth.

That was how Great Aunt Grace found me a few minutes later. That was when she told me the story of Sarah Nell Dunlap, how she had become a haint, and why she haunted the Piney Grove Primitive Baptist Church.

"See, Sarah Nell, she first come around here in the spring of '93. She come as a woman of ill repute from Knoxville with this certain madam to make a living by sinful means, and the ladies felt angered that their men's attention was turned away from hearth and home. Elmer J. Hargraves was a handsome fellow and all the single ladies wanted to go courting with him, but instead of him wanting to marry up with a respectable young lady, he took a liking to Sarah Nell. The way I heard it, Elmer come 'round to the preacher of that day, the Reverend Edward P. Hobart, father of the Prophet Hobart. Elmer asked the Reverend Edward to let him and Sarah Nell get married right here in the church. The Reverend said no—that it wasn't fitting for a man to marry with a prostitute and right out in the church house, too. Then the Lady White Caps, well, they heard tell of it, and they laid a bundle of hickory switches at Sarah Nell's front door with a note telling her to leave or else get a strict beating."

"Who were the Lady White Caps?" I asked.

"They were this group of women vigilantes that wore white masks and hats to disguise themselves. They did what was called 'rough music' or charivari attack."

"What was that?"

"Well, if any woman did something sinful, the Lady White Caps would come along and give her a warning first. If the warning didn't do no good, then they would do bodily harm. And that's what happened to Sarah Nell. See, Sarah Nell didn't leave town. She was determined to marry Elmer. So the Lady White Caps joined up with some men who egged them on, all of them disguised in the masks and hats. They all rode up to the brothel house late of an evening, dragged Sarah Nell outside and started to beating on her. The story goes that they gouged both her eyes out with a hickory stick. Ever since, Sarah Nell has been haunting this church where she hoped to get married, and she usually appears to young girls right around your age."

I squinted and looked hard at Great Aunt Grace. "You mean they killed her?"

"They did," she said. "They thought they had a right to do it because she was a woman of ill repute."

"But she didn't seem full of the devil or of ill repute when I saw her, " I said. "She just seemed lost."

"She was lost, I guess," Aunt Grace said. "The way I heard it, she wanted to quit her wicked ways, live a good life and be a wife and mama. Still, the prophet says we got to cast her haint out of this church house before she gets into somebody and takes them over."

"You think she could get into me?" I asked. "Could she get into me since I'm the one who saw her tonight and she spoke to me?"

I slept with a light on after that. I put my Bible, the little white one my grandmother gave me, under my pillow, too. I made the sign of the cross over my bed every single night and I prayed, "God, please don't let the haint get into me. Please don't let her take me over." I said the Lord's Prayer every night, and if I messed up even one word, then I went back and said it over again from scratch properly three more times in a row since three is the special number of the Father, Son, and Holy Ghost.

Everything went on as usual. Lottie and I walked to school and back every day until spring planting time came on. We rambled along the turnpike road, taking side excursions to the woods or into the fields to catch butterflies. I helped Mother shell beans on cloudy days and hang clothes on the line on clear days. And every Sunday we went to church. And every Sunday, the prophet spoke of the Outcasting that was to take place soon.

It was on a Wednesday night, the 13th of April, when the Outcasting finally happened. Everyone in town showed up at the church, everybody except, strangely enough, the two elderly ladies who always sat together on the front pew near the altar, Miss Addie Thompson and Miss Catacomb Reed.

There was a brief hymn singing, then Prophet Hobart felt the Ghost come on him and began speaking in tongues: "Hunda la shunda la! Bega ma sha. Bega ma sha lomda! Una ba sha. Talé sini mora! Sini mora! Phor seshie tara mora, Sarah Nell Dunlap! Hallelujah!"

The discernment fell on him right afterwards and he interpreted the language of the angels that he just spoke: "Haint! You evil spirit! We bind you. We bind you up! We cast you out. In the name of Jesus, turn out! Get back to the gates of hell, Sarah Nell Dunlap! Hallelujah!"

Then the prophet declared the church house was clean. The church house was free. The spirit of the haint was gone forever, relinquished back to the depths of hell where she belonged. And don't you know it was ten years later on her death bed that my Great Aunt Grace told me that Miss Addie Thompson and Miss Catacomb Reed were members of the Lady White Caps and that the prophet's own father, Reverend Edward P. Hobart, was one of the men who rode with them that night and did the dirty deed of killing poor Sarah Nell and gouging out both her eyes? And don't you know the reason he did it was because he was one of the men who took up with Sarah Nell and visited her regularly at the brothel? And don't you know that the outcasting didn't do a blessed thing? Sarah Nell Dunlap still walks down that aisle at twilight time. Why, I heard it on good authority that another young girl just coming of age saw her only last week.

PATTY IRELAND *holds a master's degree in creative writing from the University of Tennessee Knoxville and is associate professor of English at Pellissippi State Community College, where she directs its Young Creative Writer's Workshop. In addition to writing fiction and* *poetry, Ireland is a lyricist/composer. Her work has appeared in* Still: The Journal, 100 Days in Appalachia's "Creators and Innovators," *and* Appalachia Bare, *among others. She is currently writing a novel and a debut memoir entitled* East Ridge As Eden, *which chronicles her story of growing up with a mother who suffered from early-onset Alzheimer's disease and an uneducated but wise Appalachian father.*

— FOUR —

FRIEND GHOST

Knoxville, Tennessee

ELEANOR SCOTT

When we bought the house no one had touched it since the old man died.

He left a refrigerator full of rotting food, onions sprouting through their net bag on the counter. Moldy towels hung in the bathroom; a Sunday outfit hung on a hook.

The small, dilapidated house sat on the end of a working-class block of the Parkridge neighborhood in East Knoxville. The house contained dusty furniture, an unmade bed, and a gun under piles of clothes in the dresser. Pill bottles scattered everywhere. Roaches skittered everywhere, thriving.

He only lived there for one year, the last year of his life. The neighbors said he was an interior designer who claimed to have designed palaces for Saddam Hussein's family. In the attic we found his sketchbooks filled with drawings of opulent rooms so different from the rooms in which he spent his last days. He suffered from alcoholism, the neighbors said, and it eventually killed him. His name was Mel.

Mel inherited the house from his father, an auto mechanic named Hill. Hill lived in the house for more than fifty years and died there a few months before his 100th birthday.

Once, at work, I found myself chatting with a customer who lived in Parkridge as a child in the 1960s. He remembered Hill as "the old man living in the little house on the corner."

Hill would have been in his fifties then. He was the "old man on the corner" for a long time. Slowly, the house crumbled around him. He repaired everything, from broken mirrors to plumbing leaks, with duct tape.

I thought the place was beautiful and only saw potential.

I had a vision of the tiny house as a jewel box, full of beautiful polished wood, stained glass transoms, lovely antique fixtures, a window seat in the kitchen, open shelves displaying beautiful vintage dishes, hand-painted tile, a clawfoot tub in the bathroom. The fact that it had none of those things barely registered. My house was a dream house.

We had almost no money, so I planned to find everything cheap and second-hand and do the work piecemeal. I would point to a corner of rotten floorboard, daylight filtering in through cracks in the wall, and explain to friends that this is where my handmade kitchen counter, my vintage sink, was going to be. They would cough on clouds of plaster dust and look at me with wide, disbelieving eyes. But it did happen. It took two years.

We gutted the whole house and rebuilt it in our unskilled way. We picked out doors at salvage yards for their beautiful carved wood and beveled glass. Then we made them fit with handmade door frames. Sometimes, as we sat at the kitchen table, one of the doors would blow open.

"Hello, Friend Ghost," my children would say.

I had two children, ages three and five, when we moved in. They talked to Friend Ghost a lot. They did not seem afraid. Sometimes they bossed Friend Ghost around.

In movies, dogs and children can see ghosts that grownups can't. The two men who lived and died in the house were both Black and elderly.

"What does Friend Ghost look like?" I asked.

Two sets of blue eyes turned to me.

"Exactly like you, Mommy."

I felt a chill then.

We meant the house to be a starter home for our young family. We bought it cheap and fixed it up like children building a playhouse. We expected to outgrow it and move on.

A few months after we moved in, my marriage fell apart, but I stayed in the little house on the corner. Fourteen years have passed and I'm still here, writing this at the kitchen table. I tell people I can't afford to move. That's not quite true. My hand is inside a trap, clutching a beautiful jewel. I have not, so far, been able to let it go.

Sometimes I am afraid I'll never leave.

ELEANOR SCOTT *lives in the East Knoxville neighborhood of Parkridge. She worked in independent bookstores and wrote for Knoxville's alternative newspapers,* Metro Pulse, The Knoxville Mercury, *and* Compass. *Her work explores forgotten places, untold stories, and unusual lives thriving in the margins of the city. She co-owns the weird fiction small press, Part Flamingo.*

— FIVE —

THE GIRL AT UNION STATION
Erie, Pennsylvania

REGINA ZEYZUS

Chris Sirianni never believed in ghosts, never thought about ghosts, and certainly never intended to incorporate ghosts into his business plan for The Brewerie at Union Station in Erie, Pennsylvania. Then things, well, happened.

When Sirianni opened his brewpub in 2006, people told him the story of a young girl named Clara, about nine or ten years old, traveling with her parents from the art deco train depot, which originally covered two city blocks and was dedicated in 1927.

After purchasing tickets, the family exited the rotunda

with their luggage to the marble stairs leading to the train platforms. Upon reaching the top, the father turned around to check on his daughter and inadvertently hit her with his suitcase, knocking the child backwards down the stairs.

It ended the worst way possible.

Many say Clara hasn't left Union Station. Giggles, a ball rolling itself down the hallway, a girl saying someone's name, even playful tripping indicate the presence of an unseen young spirit having a bit of fun.

"Everything is like a childish prank," Sirianni says. "Nothing evil."

The tripping happens as servers walk past the foot of Clara's stairwell and enter the rotunda.

"When you walk out into this space a lot of times you feel a physical sensation on your shin, and I would say it's like a little kid sticking their foot out to trip you," Sirianni says. "You stumble a little from the sensation, then you look around to see if anyone saw."

Sirianni laughed when he first heard this from former tenants and servers. Then it started happening to him. Dozens of times later, he still laughs but out of a sense of play, not disbelief.

Almost two dozen paranormal teams have run investigations at The Brewerie, and almost all have reported the presence of a child. Psychics have repeatedly touched on the name Clara. Psychics and mediums have described impressions of a young, dark-haired girl dressed in old-fashioned clothes. A medium who gives readings during Halloween tours acknowledged that Clara is looking down into the rotunda from the balcony.

A child's giggling has been recorded as an electronic voice phenomena. "Help me" has also been heard, but Sirianni doesn't know why Clara would ask for help. Recently recorded was a voice saying, "What's that?"

Female servers have heard a young girl calling their names in the original restroom area. The spooky part is when this happens to a woman when no other women are on duty for the night.

Most hauntings occur around the rotunda, the concourse, and the second floor hallway, with a few exceptions. Ghost tours of The Brewerie include a visit to the now-unused 100-year-old tunnels beneath the station. In Union Station's prime, they were used to transfer luggage from the trains and to transport mail from the post office on the next block. One tunnel extends all the way to the Lake Erie waterfront for the transport of goods and merchandise. Off one of the large, dark, creepy tunnels is a large, dark, creepy room. Within five minutes of entering this room, electrical equipment goes dead. Batteries completely lose their charge. Sirianni says the public is no longer taken there during tours.

Another room in the tunnels was made into a bomb shelter in the 1960s. It is still stocked with decades-old gold tins of U.S. Civil Defense All-Purpose Survival Crackers. Sirianni's wife, who also didn't believe in the supernatural, was taking some family on a tour of the shelter when a tin flew off the shelf, sailed straight across the four-foot-wide tunnel, hit the wall and fell to the floor. The clanging was outdone by the screaming and the running.

A banquet room on the second floor used to be an office. Ghost investigations have recorded a man with a German accent saying, "Get out!" Thermal imaging in the banquet room has shown the outline of a person sitting in a chair when no person was sitting there. No live person, that is.

Dogs seem to be aware of something unusual, too. The Brewerie hosts Yappy Hour in the summer for customers and their dogs at their outside bar at the train platform. The dogs aren't allowed to walk through the restaurant to Clara's stairwell to get to the platform, so they get to the outside by going up a staircase from the foyer, through the hallway and on to the platform. The dogs are fine and well-behaved in the foyer and up the stairs, then go bonkers in the hallway, barking with excitement. They go back to being fine and well-behaved outside. There is something, or someone, in the hallway that gets the dogs all excited. It is a happy, playful excitement, not fearful. Could it be the spirit of a playful child?

Sirianni says no one has been able to document the death of a child named Clara at Union Station. Many paranormal investigators have done library research without success. Maybe Clara isn't the child's given name, maybe it's a nickname or her middle name. Or maybe the issue of the local newspaper recording her death wasn't archived.

Formal documentation may be lacking, but one last piece of this ghostly puzzle could change anyone's mind about Clara.

While preparing to open for the public years ago, Sirianni and his IT guy worked at the station at night after their day jobs. Sometimes the IT guy would be on babysitting duty and bring his four-year-old daughter with him. She would quietly go off and play by herself. One night Sirianni went home early and asked the IT guy to close up when he left.

The next day, he told Sirianni that when it was time to leave, he found his daughter and asked if she was ready to go. She looked at him square in the eye and said, "Dad, hold on, I have to say good-bye to my friend. She fell down the stairs."

There were no other children there, no other people.

After eighteen years of strange happenings, Sirianni is open to the possibility that there are more things in the natural world than we're taught to believe.

"Something goes on here," he says. "It's hard to deny. I was a nonbeliever and now like I've done a 180."

REGINA ZEYZUS *has been reading ghost stories since she was old enough to hold a book. Unfortunately, she seems to be as psychic as a potato and has never seen a ghost herself. Her background is in chemistry, geology, and technical editing. She lives in Southwestern New York with four cats, and she collects vintage cookbooks and short horror stories.*

— SIX —

DREAD, BEAUTY, AND TRAGEDY COME IN PINK

Wellsville, New York

BRAD LIFFORD

Some earthly forms possess a magnetic beauty that lures the gaze. People can hold this power—and stately homes, too. The Pink House, a Victorian manor in Wellsville, New York, is such a house. In this small town in the Southern Tier, the three-story structure is painted bright pink, with ornate trim work and a striking front tower that looms above all who pass by.

The Pink House has dominated the corner of State Street and Brooklyn Avenue since it was built in 1868. Stories about ghosts who reside there—spirits anchored by tragedy, including the death of a child—have captured the public's imagination.

Those stories bring people to Wellsville to see the Pink House. The locals know the stories. Some know them all too well—from indelible experience.

Having passed by the Pink House a thousand times, Michael Flanagan could resist staring. He lived across the street and could see the house anytime from his bedroom window. And ghosts? They weren't on his mind as he walked up the street on a November afternoon. The fourteen-year-old was going to see his girl.

But on this day, there would be no ignoring the Pink House.

As he drew up in front of the house, he suddenly stopped. Out of the corner of his eye, he had seen something. Something moving. Something dark. The hair on his neck raised, prickling his skin. He smelled a strange odor. Ozone, he thought.

Something felt wrong.

Michael turned and fully took in the Pink House, vibrant and inviting on that sunny, cool day. His gaze lifted upward to the two ornate windows in the high tower.

Through the glass, he saw the silhouette of a woman. She wore a long dress, and Michael could see its full drape, down to the hem, as if she were suspended above the floor. And she was suspended, he saw. The woman hung from the ceiling on a rope. Like the sway of a pendulum, she moved back and forth, from one window to the next.

Down below, the boy's heart raced. He stared a few seconds to be sure his eyes weren't playing tricks. Dangling, the woman continued to sway from side to side.

Though he had so far lived his life fearlessly, growing up on a farm, camping in the woods by himself at night, listening to hard stories told by his police officer father, the boy was shaken by what he saw.

Michael turned and ran up the sidewalk.

"I don't believe in ghosts."

More than thirty years have passed, and the teenager from Wellsville is now a man in his forties, sitting at a table more than one thousand miles south at his brewery in Kingsport, Tennessee. He pauses for a couple of seconds.

"Wait. I shouldn't put it like that," Michael says.

He goes on. What he believes in are rational explanations for things that invite mystery. A moan then the creak of stairs in the middle of the night can be wind and a settling foundation. The appearance of an apparition on a darkened night? The interplay of light and fog or mist.

"I guess I should say I'm skeptical," he continues, "because I believe with most stuff like that, there's a rational explanation for what happened."

Michael Flanagan cannot explain the Pink House. Cannot forget the woman he saw through the window, nor the other experience that shook and still shakes his otherwise firm belief in rationality.

Built by pharmacist Edwin B. Hall, the Pink House has long been the touchstone of Wellsville, once a thriving mill town. Perhaps its mysteries are in part due to the fact that most who experience the house do so only from without. It isn't a museum; it isn't a rental property where the curious can stay overnight—the Pink House has been in the same family since its beginning, having been passed down through five generations of the family line. It has always been a private residence, though not always a primary residence. It's sometimes unoccupied and pristine, only a caretaker tending things from a guest house. The Pink House often rests through days and nights alone, mostly without a human presence but for the memories of lives lived and all the associated family laughter, drama, joy, and tears that accumulate through the passage of years. And, unfortunately, the memory of at least one family tragedy.

In the early 1900s, a two-year-old girl wandered out of the house and drowned in a fountain on the grounds. Historical reports indicate this death was compounded by another form of tragedy: The girl's grandfather saw this happen from the front porch, and could not save her because he was confined to a wheelchair.

Another legend that persists through the years is that visitors standing on the front porch can hear a rhythmic creaking from the floor of the porch—a ghostly echo of the grandfather frantically moving to and fro, desperate to prevent the drowning but unable to do so.

Another death that believers attribute to the Pink House—of a love-stricken woman, Mary Frances Farnum, who committed suicide—actually did not occur at the Pink House. She reportedly drowned herself in 1857—and her ghost, some say, lured the two-year-old to her death by drowning almost fifty years later.

The current owner, Jay Woelful, is intrigued by the folk stories that have grown up around the family house, though he would prefer the manor be appreciated for its lovely architecture and deep history. Though private, the Pink House is embedded in the community: The owners decorate the house for Halloween and welcome trick-or-treaters. When a local historian wrote about the house, public talks on its history and architecture were held there.

William Paquette co-authored *The Pink House* with the late Dr. Julian B. Woelfel, who once owned it. Paquette was resolute that it was a history book, not a ghost book: This is a ghost-free tour, he wrote. The Pink House never had ghosts.

That sums up the view of Jay Woelful, who—in a twist of irony—is a maker of horror movies. He even filmed one of his movies there, and has a favorite story he wishes were true: That bloody bats have been known to fly up out of an old well on the grounds. The stories of Pink House mysteries persist, and Woelful sometimes engages in the Internet posts recounting ghostly experiences with gentle comments that correct reports with what he knows: There was no death by hanging at the Pink House. The house has a rich history, but it is not haunted.

On the topic of ghosts in general, Michael Flanagan would mostly agree. Mostly.

He explains why his resolute statement from earlier—I don't believe in ghosts—comes with a caveat.

It is some thirty years later after he saw the ghastly silhouette in that window. Around the corner from the table hangs a framed, black-and-white photo of that house. He continues toward reconciliation of his disbelief in the supernatural, the Pink House aside.

"I guess I should say I'm skeptical," he continues, "because I believe with most stuff like that, there's a good, rational explanation for what happened."

Michael Flanagan will never be able to explain the Pink House.

Never forget or explain what he saw in the window—when he fled to his girlfriend's house, they went back and saw nothing. He talked to the caretakers, who told him no one had been inside the house's uppermost room, cleaning windows.

"I know what I saw," he says.

Michael also cannot forget when he and his sister, both not yet ten years old, saw a young girl in dress of Victorian times, walking slowly and gracefully through the front yard. Yearning for another playmate, they called to her and invited her over. She did not respond. She kept walking, and the two young Flanagans watched her stride without pause into a large bush. They never saw her emerge.

And then, there was his last brush with the Pink House.

"I was a volunteer firefighter," he remembers. "I was close to graduating from high school, and I already knew I wanted to be a firefighter someday.

"There was no one living in the house at the time, and we got a call that a smoke alarm was going off inside the Pink House. We got the call to go check it out."

He and a friend, Mark, traveled to the house. The caretakers let them in. They saw no fire. To be thorough, they moved up the winding staircase that ascended three flights to the looming tower.

They made it to the second landing and stopped—but not by choice. As if his boots were pinned to the stairstep by some great, unseen hand, Michael could not move his feet.

He had just bounded up two flights, eager to make it to the top and confirm that this fire call was a false alarm. Now his heartbeat raced.

"My feet won't move—I can't go up," he said. Mark, also dressed in firefighter gear, was right behind him. "I can't move either," he told Michael.

Trying harder to move proved fruitless. The only way they could move—were allowed to move—was back down the stairs. After another minute, they retreated back down.

They left the house. On the drive back to the fire station, they didn't know what to say. They felt helpless and disconcerted. How could something they could not see pin them to the floor? They were dumbstruck.

And, the two young men were scared. That feeling never went away.

"We were there in Wellsville a few years ago," Flanagan says. He still keeps memories of Wellsville close, still has relatives there, still returns to maintain those ties.

This visit was an opportunity for his children to see his hometown and the places frequented as he grew up. Places like the David A. Howe Public Library, The Famous Texas Hot, his family farm. They all wanted to go to the Pink House.

All except one.

"I told them they could go if they wanted," Michael says. He smiles gently and shakes his head. "I'll never go near that house again."

BRAD LIFFORD *is a co-founder of Howling Hills Publishing.*

— SEVEN —

A Promise that Haunts Through the Ages

Plymouth Township, Pennsylvania

THOM TRACY

Willie Hatton's father made a promise. Thomas Hatton would show his ten-year-old son where he worked from sunup to sundown. That's why the two ventured far into the depths of a coal mine in the Avondale section of Plymouth Township, Pennsylvania on September 6, 1869. For Willie, it may have been an opportunity to see how Papa managed to put bread on the table—most of the time, that is.

Just ten days earlier, miners and the Delaware, Lackawanna, and Western Railroad, which owned the mine, had settled a three-month strike. Tensions were still high and safety conditions lacking. It was the early days of anthracite mining and rough-hewn timber lined the shaft that plunged 327 feet straight into the ground. Way down there, fathers dug coal alongside their sons. Miners got dragged and dropped into the hole on a rickety platform, raised and lowered by ropes connected to a team of horses plodding in circles. The sole entrance was the only way into the mine. And there was no other way out. England had outlawed single-shaft mines but in the United States, no such ban existed.

That proved fatal when a fire ignited in the belly of the mine and seared its way up the shaft's bratticed walls. Investigators labeled it an accident, triggered by embers from a smaller, regulated fire in a furnace designed to create drafts to facilitate air circulation. But on the heels of the organized work stoppage, arson had also been suspected as a cause, with payback considered a motive.

The inferno raged to the surface and consumed a colliery atop the entrance. Parts of the building collapsed into the shaft. Since no alternate escape route or proper ventilation outlets existed, the fire above sucked all the breathable air from the tunnels. Soon charred debris blocked access to the shaft. Poisonous gases sought out every man and boy no matter where they sought shelter. The toxic fumes killed 108 souls below and two people attempting to rescue them.

No one underground cheated death that day. These men and boys—those fathers and sons—would be memorialized in a mournful ballad. One verse reads:

The women and their children,
Their hearts were filled with joy,
To see their men go to their work
Likewise every boy;
But a dismal sight in broad daylight,
Soon made them turn pale,
When they saw the breaker burning
O'er the mines of Avondale.

Northeastern Pennsylvania was once the nucleus of the anthracite coal mining industry. This corner of the Commonwealth—two hours north of Philadelphia and two hours west of New York City—held greater reserves of the slow-burning anthracite than anywhere else in the world. The departed industry still graces the region's Wyoming Valley and its residents with mine subsidence, polluted soil and water—and maybe the presence of restless spirits.

The site of the former Avondale coal mine rests above the banks of the Susquehanna River in Plymouth Township, a ten-minute drive from Wilkes-Barre. One hundred and fifty-five years after the catastrophe, it seems there are those who still yearn for infinite sleep. To this day, visitors report strange phenomena. The mine entrance has been sealed for decades but phantoms appear to have made their way to the surface.

In 2022, paranormal researchers descended on the site. They'd heard about feelings of dread on the grounds and cold currents of air from a vent near the mouth of the plugged-up mine. They shot video and snapped photos. On closer inspection, one exposure showed the image of a young, fair-haired boy—the sort of revelation they hoped for.

Thinking the camera captured ghostly looking leaves or litter, a team member headed back to the mine. At the spot where the image presented itself, no trash or tree branches or brush existed. The ghost hunter discovered nothing in the physical realm that could be mistaken for a young boy's apparition.

In 1869, those spearheading the recovery efforts remarked on the positions of the lifeless bodies found in the passageways. The skin of the victims had turned crimson, a sign the men and boys had been deprived of oxygen. Some sat with eyes open and backs against the chamber walls. Others moved to build barricades in isolated pockets, hundreds of feet from the main shaft. They had been found in stages of undress. To prevent the deadly gas clouds from entering the space, the doomed miners stuffed their clothing into cracks in the barricade walls.

The fire may have been an intentional act or the result of ownership negligence. We'll never know for sure. The official report detailing the scene states one fact with certainty: Deep within the motherlode, a miner was found with his arms around a very young boy.

THOM TRACY *writes business articles and blog posts for investment sites, insurance businesses, and software companies. He is the author of* The Kings of Cork Lane, *a memoir about family and friends written through a baseball lens. He lives in West Pittston, Pennsylvania, and enjoys bicycling and collecting pre-war baseball cards.*

— EIGHT —

THE BLOODY SEVENTH
Hancock County, Tennessee

DANITA DODSON

In my grandmother's day, the Hancock County district where she was born and raised was dubbed "The Bloody Seventh." The official place-name of the community was "Big Creek," derived from the large creek that flows through expansive fields and into the nearby Clinch River. According to a local legend, a man was riding his horse near Big Creek as the day was growing dusky dark. Shot by someone who waylaid him in the woods, the victim was suspended upside down from the saddle as his horse pulled him through the creek. As people once remembered, "The creek water looked like pure blood flowing, where the horse had torn him to pieces as it dragged him." Some say this event was the origin of the name "The Bloody Seventh." But most people in this East Tennessee community still claim the moniker was a commentary on the widespread lawlessness and the numerous murders that were once committed here. Many have never been solved.

My grandmother was present when one of these murders occurred on August 7, 1921. She was a seven-old-year girl at the time. "Mamaw Velvie," as she was known to me, was a bubbling fountain of stories about local history. Though she told me many tales, some of her greatest storytelling focused upon her memories of Bill Blake, a man who gained notoriety as a murderer in the Bloody Seventh community. A larger-than-life character in local legends, he even supposedly haunted the house where he had once lived and died.

Below is an interview I did with my grandmother about the Bloody Seventh, Bill Blake, and his haunted house. It appears in her own words as she told it to me many years ago.

Back when I was growing up as a girl in the early 1920s, our part of the county was called the Bloody Seventh. I guess it earned its name on account of the many killings that took place here. I remember Mama telling me about when Uncle Henley Sutton was shot while he was out under a tree drinking, but he wasn't bothering anybody. And they say Joshua Dodson was sitting out on his front porch one evening, minding his own business, for he was an old feeble man, when somebody shot him and tried to pack it off on another fellow.

Those aren't the only killings that happened around here. I could name many more. Killing was common in those days. And as I was just a little girl then, I was often scared. Why, ever man I knew packed a gun with him anywhere he went, even to church! If a man ever got to fighting with another one, he might get so mad and just pull out that gun and shoot him. And many did just that. To them shooting was the only way to settle anything. And the law never bothered to come around. Mama said they were scared to. Only one man that I ever heard tell of went to the pen for killing a man, cutting him up into little pieces, and burning the pieces in a church-house stove.

But there's one killing that sticks in my mind because I was there when it happened. Now I didn't see it firsthand because I was inside the church house, but I heard a lot of people talking about it. Even though I was a little bitty girl, I recollect what I saw and what they said.

Bill Blake and his boy Car had come down to Ida's Chapel where the church was holding a funeral for Jack Stanifer. After the funeral was over, some people were standing on the outside, and Mart Lewis was one of them. They say Bill and Car came especially to kill Mart, and sure enough old Mart was shot and killed. I didn't see them shoot him, but I recollect seeing Vad Lewis, Mart's wife, running back down to the church screaming. Her hands were all bloody where she had touched Mart.

Everybody knew it was going to happen. I mean, they knew Bill or Car would soon shoot old Mart if somebody didn't beat them to it. You see, the Lewises and the Blakes go back a long way. They started a feud over some ducks. I don't rightly know how or why they fought over ducks, but I know that ducks were part of the feuding. Fact of the matter is the Lewises were bothering Bill or Car about something all the time.

But the way I see it, Bill and Car Blake wouldn't harm anybody. I don't see how they could have shot Mart. Bill Blake was a good man. I know because I lived close to him when I was a kid, and Mama would often take me to his house. Why, he even gave me some candy and pennies whenever I saw him! And Bill's wife Mary was always good to me. She'd take baskets of food to anybody who'd get sick, and I was one of the sickest of them. I was so sick as a girl that Granny Winkler prayed for me to die, but Bill's wife prayed for me to live.

The law never did anything about Mart's killing, but people counted Bill and Car as mean men. Long after the killing, when Bill was dead himself, lots of people told that Bill and Car was absolutely not the ones who did it. You see, a lot of people on the outside of the church saw the whole thing and was hissing it up, wanting Bill and Car to kill Mart because nobody liked him. Maybe everybody told that it was Bill and Car who were the murderers because they were the ones that seemed to have the most against Mart and would be good ones to pack it off on.

Well, after Bill Blake died, people began to tell that his old house was haunted. They said you could hear him playing his fiddle late at night. And people were scared to buy that old house and move in, mostly because they thought Bill Blake was a mean man when he was alive, and they didn't want to meet him when he was dead.

Elmo and I moved into Bill's house in 1946 when we left the holler. We became sharecroppers who tended the land where the vacated house sat. Our employer let us live there without paying rent. We didn't believe there was a haint in the house.

But pretty soon though, we began to hear a fiddle playing late at night. At least we thought we did. Now, since nobody in our house knew how to play a fiddle, we knew something funny was going on. I'd put my two babies to bed at night, but my little Clarence would wiggle and cry over hearing that old fiddle playing. We got tired of hearing it and commenced to believe what people were saying about a haint in Bill Blake's house.

Then one night Clarence just wouldn't stop crying because he said somebody was playing a fiddle outside and wouldn't let him sleep. So I went over to the window to see what was the matter. I opened it and felt a strong wind blowing. Outside the window was a tall pear tree that leaned against the house. Well, then I thought I heard the fiddle even closer. I really thought Bill Blake's ghost just might be sitting in that there tree. But when I stuck my head out of that window, I saw what was making them say it was a fiddle. A long branch on that old tree was rubbing against the house in a way that was causing it to sound like string music.

The next day I had Elmo to cut that old branch off, and we never heard the fiddle again.

DANITA DODSON *is an educator, literary scholar, and the author of three poetry collections,* Trailing the Azimuth (2021), The Medicine Woods (2022), *and* Between Gone and Everlasting (2024). *She is also the co-editor of the book* Teachers Teaching Nonviolence (2020). *Dodson's poems have appeared in* Salvation South, Amethyst Review, Heimat Review, Braided Way, Jarfly Poetry Magazine, Tennessee Voices Anthology, *and elsewhere. She is a native of Sneedville, Tennessee, where she hikes and explores local history connected to the wilderness. Read more at www.danitadodson.com.*

— NINE —

WHERE'S DENNIS?

Cades Cove, Tennessee

JENNIE IVEY

It began as nothing more than a light-hearted game of hide-and-seek, played by four little boys on a picture-perfect summer afternoon in the Great Smoky Mountains National Park. The youngest boy wore a bright red T-shirt. "Go hide over there, Dennis, away from us," the others told him, pointing to a nearby tangle of mountain laurel and rhododendrons. "You're too easy to spot in that shirt."

Dennis grinned and quickly obeyed.

The adults who'd gathered for a picnic near the Spence Field shelter, a popular spot for thru-hikers on the

Appalachian Trail, smiled and pretended not to notice the boys were hiding. When three boys dashed out of the woods to scare them, the grown-ups shrieked in mock surprise. Everyone laughed uproariously.

A few minutes passed, but Dennis didn't emerge from his hiding place.

"Hey, bud," his dad hollered, heading toward the wooded area where he'd last seen his son. "Come on out. We're getting ready to eat." But Dennis didn't show. Not then. Not ever. More than fifty years later, what happened to young Dennis Martin on June 14, 1969, is a Smoky Mountain mystery that's never been solved.

Some say his ghost still haunts those hills.

Father's Day weekend of 1969 was to be a special one for the Martin family of Knoxville, Tennessee. Their kinfolk had settled in Cades Cove in the 1800s and had grazed cattle and sheep for decades on the man-made bald known as Spence Field. With the creation of the national park in 1934, the family relocated. But they never stopped spending time in their beloved mountains.

As part of a long family tradition, three generations of Martin men planned to celebrate Father's Day weekend, which began on Friday the Thirteenth, in the park.

For the first time ever, six-year-old Dennis—who was quick to remind everyone he'd be turning seven the next week—would join his nine-year-old brother Douglas, their dad Bill, and granddad Clyde to hike and camp near where the state lines of Tennessee and North Carolina come together, just south of Cades Cove. On Friday, as planned, the foursome spent the night at Russell Field. After a hearty breakfast Saturday morning, they headed east to Spence Field, where others were to join them for a picnic later in the day.

Dennis had no trouble traversing the three miles to Spence Field, which towers almost 5,000 feet above sea level. He'd traveled Smoky Mountain trails all his life, some even before he could walk, secure in a pack strapped to his father's strong shoulders. Dennis was small for his age, four feet tall and weighing only fifty-three pounds as his seventh birthday approached, but strong and fit. And he was absolutely unafraid of the wilderness. "Slow down!" his parents would holler whenever he got too far ahead of them on a trail. "You're just a little boy. We need to keep an eye on you!"

Now, in a nightmare worse than any they could have imagined, Dennis had vanished.

Bill began running down the trail near where the boys had been playing, trying to control the panic in his voice as he yelled his son's name over and over and over again. The other adults fanned out in all directions, doing the same. There was no answer. And no sign of the brown-eyed, brown-haired boy in the red shirt. As darkness fell, Clyde set off for the nearest ranger station—nine miles away in Cades Cove—to report his grandson missing.

Then the storm rolled in.

Winds blew. Lightning flashed and thunder rolled. The temperature dropped to fifty degrees. Rain fell in buckets, more than three inches in just a few hours, turning trails to mud and streams into raging rivers that overflowed their banks. Searching for Dennis at night in such weather would be futile. His family could only hope and pray he'd found a cave to crawl into and stay dry.

Naturally, no one slept that night. At first light, the search began again. And what a search it was. As news about Dennis's disappearance spread, hundreds of people swarmed the Great Smoky Mountains National Park to look for him. Within days, the search would become the most massive manhunt in park history.

In addition to park rangers and professional trackers, National Guardsmen joined the effort. So did Green Berets and Boy Scouts and psychics and backcountry woodsmen and a whole host of well-meaning people who knew absolutely nothing about the wilderness or about search and rescue. The lost boy in the Smokies made international headlines. Within days, the number of people who showed up to "help" grew to about 1,400.

Any evidence that might have existed was likely destroyed by massive crowds and bad weather. As days passed with no sign of Dennis, park officials shook their heads in despair and began to watch for buzzards. "It will take nothing short of a miracle to find the boy," one of them said. The $5,000 reward offered by the Martin family yielded no leads.

On June 29, two weeks after Dennis went missing, the search for him was officially abandoned.

So what happened to Dennis Martin? Theories abound. The most probable explanation, according to park officials, is that

Dennis—lost and afraid and exposed to the elements—died quickly of exposure. Footprints that may have belonged to him led to a swollen stream and then disappeared. He could have fallen into that stream and been swept away. He could have stumbled off a high cliff. He could have been killed, and perhaps eaten, by wild hogs or coyotes or black bears that inhabit the Smokies in large numbers.

Sixteen years after Dennis disappeared, a man claimed that—while hunting ginseng in the late fall of 1985—he had come across a small human skeleton. He failed to report it in a timely manner because ginseng harvesting is illegal and he didn't want to go to jail. A search of the area in question found no human remains.

There are those who believe Dennis was snatched by a bad guy in the park, though no evidence of such an abduction has ever been uncovered. And a handful of folks swear that "feral people" who live deep in the most remote areas of the Smokies—their existence, of course, kept secret by park officials—kidnapped Dennis on that fateful June evening and raised him as their own child. He may, they suggest, still be part of the tribe today.

The National Center for Missing and Exploited Children released an age-progression photo that shows what Dennis might look like as a fifty-something-year-old man, but no one has ever reported seeing him. The little boy's disappearance is a cold case that continues to baffle everyone who knows about it.

"It's likely impossible we'll ever find out what happened to Dennis Martin," a park official said. "It's one of the saddest and most-enduring mysteries of the Smokies."

But is Dennis really gone?

Perhaps not. To this day, tourists at the visitor's center in Cades Cove occasionally report seeing a small, dark-haired boy wearing a red T-shirt standing alone and looking lost and afraid.

At the Tipton Place on the Cades Cove loop, some visitors swear they feel a strange cool breeze—even in high summer—and that the hair on the back of their necks stands up as they draw near the cabin. That cabin was featured in the 1984 movie "The Dollmaker," based upon the beloved 1954 novel by Appalachian writer Harriet Arnow. In it, sharecropper Gertie Nevels longs to buy a house of her own. The dreamed-about house featured in the movie is actually the Tipton cabin in Cades Cove. And, like Dennis's parents, Gertie and her husband lose their six-year-old child in a tragic accident.

Coincidence? Maybe so, maybe not.

Most spooky and unexplainable of all are photos that have been taken near the Tipton cabin. They show what appears to be a small, shadowy figure at the edge of the woods. Is it merely the sun and clouds playing tricks? Is it simply part of a tree? Or might it be the apparition of a little boy, perhaps the little boy who went missing way back on Father's Day weekend in 1969, simply looking for a warm, dry place to lay his head?

JENNIE IVEY *has written more than a thousand columns for the* Herald-Citizen *in Cookeville, Tennessee, and is the author of two books about Tennessee History and one about Elvis. She's a regular contributor to* Guideposts *publications and to the* Chicken Soup for the Soul *collections.*

— TEN —

I CARRIED THE SIGHT

Ducktown, Tennessee

SUE WEAVER DUNLAP

I hid out deep in my mama as long as I could, loathe to leave a cocoon where I eavesdropped on women who spoke in hushed voices when secrets were shared. I soaked up their words before I knew the power of language. After I was born, Mama sheltered me from mountain ways, insisting I grow up with education and culture. When I turned three, I revealed a troubling gift Mama and her sisters all had. This probably came from my great-grandmother's people, the Snowbird Cherokees.

It was late December 1956. My granddaddy Goode was in declining health because of a series of strokes. Daddy drove

Mama and me to Ducktown, Tennessee, to see him. The visit was good. I remember being in his lap as he sat near the fireplace, his long hands wrapping me close, the smell of Prince Albert cherry tobacco seeping into muscle memory. Kin sat around the front room and played music and sang ballads and hymns. I remember it was a happy time. No one talked about death. The next morning, we headed home, me standing up on the truck seat between my parents. According to Mama, I suddenly turned to Daddy and told him he had to turn back—Poppy was dead. We had to go back.

Memory is a tricky thing, especially when you are a young girl. I remember Mama putting her arms around my legs and making me sit down. I also remember her and Daddy exchanging the "parent look." However, we didn't turn back. Back then that trip from Ducktown along the Ocoee River to Highway 411 north to Knoxville took forever.

Later, Mama told how the phone was ringing when they walked in the door. Our number then was 5274. She accepted charges from the other end. Poppy had passed peacefully in his chair by the fireplace around an hour after we left, about the time I made my plea to go back.

I attended my first funeral that Christmas, though I only remember smells, the dim light around Poppy's casket, the tall people surrounding me, and hushed voices. I later learned my Aunt Mildred had the same experience as I and started packing for Ducktown immediately. Over the following few years, Mama told me repeatedly never to speak of this again and not to have any more of these "feelings."

My close kin, however, never stopped talking about it, especially the women. Always in hushed voices, the same hushed voices that connected me to them way before I was born. These premonitions or feelings or as my people called them—the sight—didn't go away. I just kept them to myself.

Mondays were always wash days at our house. After breakfast was over and Daddy left for work, we began sorting clothes. I moved the dish drainer off the top of the wringer washing machine, and Mama pushed our prized Maytag over to the white cast iron sink and connected the hoses. I brought her the Tide and bleach from the back porch, and our day began.

About mid-day on that particular summer morning, we heard a howdy from the front room. My Aunt Joyce and her son Perry were on their way from Detroit to Ducktown to visit Grandma Goode and stopped briefly to see us. When it was time for them to leave, Aunt Joyce said, "Lizzie, are you sure you don't want to go with me to see Mommy."

"No, I best not," I remember Mama saying. I didn't say anything.

About an hour after they left, Mama said, "Girl, what's wrong? You've not said ten words since Joyce left. Something eating at you?"

"You'll get mad if I tell you."

"I'll get even madder if you don't," she said. "Speak up right now."

"Grandma is sick, maybe even dead," I told her. "She's on the floor beside her bed. Something's wrong with her."

"Well, I wish you had told me before they left," she said. "We would have gone with them. Now, let's put all this away and get ready to go when your daddy gets home."

Never once did she question me about what I saw. She simply gathered some clothes and began calling around to try and find Daddy.

That afternoon Aunt Joyce called from Copper Basin Hospital. Again, Mama accepted charges. They had found Grandma unconscious on the floor beside her bed. The doctors were working with her. She might not make it.

This time, my "sight" became fodder for the entire family. My brother Leslan even told me if I ever saw anything about him to let him know and he would go to bed and hide. It was in the aftermath of this family emergency that Mama explained what was happening to me, to some of our women kin, probably inherited from great-grandmother Salina, the Cherokee.

"Best we not talk about it," Mama said.

But I did talk about it one more time. A couple of years later on February 5, my Daddy's birthday, we woke up to a light snow. It was a Saturday, back when dentists still worked on Saturday. At breakfast I told Mama I had seen Papaw Weaver early that morning in his casket. He was dressed in his only suit, the suit he always wore when he preached at the corner of Union Avenue and Market Square on Saturdays before he couldn't walk much anymore.

"We'll see," was all she said.

Of course, we didn't say anything to Daddy about such. He took me on to see Dr. Blackstock. About halfway through the appointment, Mama called the office to give us the message. Papaw Weaver had died in his sleep after the aide had taken him out to see the snow early that morning.

Over the years after that, my sight morphed into many things. I could feel Mama's pain no matter where I was. Two girl cousins and I always knew when one of us was in danger, either physically or emotionally. And my brother, the one who told me if I ever "saw" anything about him he would just go to bed, died of cancer in 1995.

SUE WEAVER DUNLAP *lives in Walland, Tennessee, on a mountain farm with her husband Raymond. Publications include* Appalachian Journal, Appalachian Heritage, Pine Mountain Sand and Gravel, Anthology of Appalachian Writers, Kakalak, *and* The Southern Poetry Anthology. *Dunlap's works also include* A Walk to the Spring House, *Iris Press (2021),* Knead, *Main Street Rag (2016), and* Story Tender, *Finishing Line Press (2014).*

No. ELEVEN

BRUSHY MOUNTAIN PRISON BLUES
Petros, Tennessee

KEVIN SAYLOR

One Sunday morning in 1997, a drifter walked into a Captain D's restaurant in the Donelson neighborhood of Nashville and shot two people. Paul Dennis Reid Jr., an aspiring country singer from Texas, was out on parole, having served seven years of a twenty-year sentence for armed robbery. Reid was then living in a boarding house in Middle Tennessee.

He had a troubled childhood. After his parents divorced, Reid went to live with his paternal grandmother. He tortured animals, bullied other children, stole cars, and attempted to murder his grandmother by setting fire to her bed while she slept.

On this particular February day, Reid convinced the Captain D's manager to let him inside to apply for a job. Instead, he forced the twenty-five-year-old and another employee, just sixteen, into the restaurant cooler at gunpoint. He made them lie face down on the frigid floor, shot them execution style, then took money from the cash register and left. He later used the stolen cash to buy a car.

Over the span of the next two months, Reid robbed two more fast food eateries and murdered five more people. His earlier stint in prison hadn't taught him repentance, but rather not to leave witnesses. He was apprehended later that year. He was tried and convicted three separate times, with each jury voting for him to receive the death penalty.

Reid was one of thousands of inmates who spent time locked in Brushy Mountain State Penitentiary in Petros, a tiny East Tennessee town in Morgan County. The maximum-security prison was the end of the line. It's where the worst of the worst offenders—murderers, rapists, armed robbers, and the like—served multiple life sentences, with no hope of ever getting out.

Brushy Mountain operated from 1896 until it closed in 2009. For those 113 years, it was a vicious place. Brushy Mountain opened in the aftermath of the Coal Creek War, a labor uprising in Briceville. Convicts worked the nearby mines and built the prison. Life was difficult; inmates were beaten for underproducing in the mines. The wooden prison was overcrowded and diseases like black lung, tuberculosis, typhoid fever, and syphilis were widespread.

The original structure was replaced in the 1920s with one that still stands, an eerie fortress made from stone quarried on the property. The convicts mined the rock to build their own prison. It was built in the shape of a Greek cross, perhaps an architectural prayer for redemption. Or a reminder that death was never far away.

The prison saw 10,000 documented deaths. Accounting for the four years the complex was closed, that comes out to ninety-one deaths a year, which averages a death every four days. The prison did not carry out executions, so those deaths either came from disease or violence.

Some were horrific. For instance, there's the tale of two inmates who stabbed a man to death in the kitchen, nearly sliced off his arm, then severed his spine with a meat cleaver. On another occasion, seven white prisoners held a guard hostage at knifepoint and took his gun. They found four black rivals and opened fire on them while they were trapped in their cells. Two died; the others survived by hiding behind mattresses.

There are stories of inmates being stabbed to death while doing pullups in the yard, of having their throats cut from ear to ear in the movie theater, of having weights pushed onto their chests while exercising and then being stabbed while pinned down.

Perhaps the prison's most famous inmate was James Earl Ray, the assassin of Martin Luther King Jr. Ray came to the prison in 1970. He made a few escape attempts before he and six others made it over a wall in 1977. He was recaptured two days later. In 1981, Ray was stabbed 22 times by three inmates. He survived and was transferred to Nashville in 1992.

In 2009 it was deemed cheaper to close Brushy Mountain and transfer prisoners elsewhere than to remodel the existing facilities or constantly repair them.

It's a soggy Saturday night in early December and Brushy Mountain looms on the horizon like a castle. The foreboding white structure sits nestled into the side of a mountain, enveloped by a thick blanket of fog. Half a dozen cars are parked in the lot outside the entrance. Despite the presence of people, the decommissioned prison feels desolate. The air is quiet, the sort of silence that feels discomforting, that makes you look over your shoulder.

I plan on spending the night.

That's because in 2018, Brushy Mountain reopened its doors to a new income stream: tourism. During normal business hours, the prison offers tours, sometimes led by former guards or prisoners themselves. After dark, tourists can hunt for ghosts. Supposedly, it's one of the most haunted places in the state.

I'm joined by ten other paranormal investigators and two guides.

We enter the prison through a derelict hallway, the yellow paint peeling, the walls riddled with what look like bullet holes. The checkered floor tile is chipped and dirty. Toward the end of the hall there's a massive gate separating the prison from the outside world. We walk through, past a small holding cell, and into an atrium where the commissary used to be. Now it's home to a machine selling overpriced bottled water and sodas. The atrium opens to the left and right, leading to the yard.

The yard is large and has basketball goals and a wooden whipping post where prisoners were chained and beaten. It's flanked by a gymnasium, D-block, and a former maximum-security unit. To the rear of the prison is a concert stage and surprisingly nice bathroom facilities. Beyond the bathrooms is a stone wall topped with barbed wire and guard towers. The fence backs into rugged, mountainous terrain. The idea was, even if prisoners managed to get over the fence, they wouldn't get far.

Our main guide tells us about the prison's history and describes the paranormal activity there. She tells us death was rampant in the prison and that in the era of segregation after Reconstruction some prisoners were incarcerated for crimes as petty and trumped up as swearing. She explains that some murders on the grounds were so savage, guards flushed what was left of victims down the toilets. She talks of whippings and beatings and sorrow.

And with so much violence, death, and injustice, if there's anywhere on earth that would house restless spirits, Brushy Mountain is the place. Our guide tells us she encounters something unusual almost every time she is here. She talks of apparitions forming right in front of your eyes, and of whispers and growls on audio recordings made on the premises. There are stories of furniture moving violently on its own, of visitors being shoved, of clothing burned by invisibile cigarettes.

After our guide finishes talking, we are on our own. For seven hours. Inside a pitch dark, former maximum-security prison. We are allowed to wander around as we please. Through the cell blocks. Into unlocked cells. Up to the edge of the guard towers. To the cafeteria. Into the gym. Through the yard. To the hole. By ourselves. With no supervision.

To reiterate, and I cannot say this enough, myself and ten strangers are wandering through a supposedly-haunted former prison where thousands died. In the dark. On a windy, rainy, stormy night. This is how horror movies begin.

I am not a squeamish person. I watched my first "Nightmare on Elm Street" movie in elementary school. I've watched countless "Friday the 13th" and "Halloween" movies. But Brushy Mountain is an unnerving place. Even if there aren't any ghosts, the grounds are so large a serial killer could come on a daytime tour and stay overnight without anyone knowing.

The halls of the prison are cramped and the layout is winding and confusing in the dark. We pass by dozens of tiny cells, most furnished with a sink, a toilet, a small desk with a stool bolted to the floor, and an uncomfortable-looking metal bed. The white paint of the cells is flaked, revealing rust underneath. The cells do not have outside windows. Exposed pipes run overhead in the halls and the floors are wet with rainwater from the storm earlier. One cell has hundreds of tally marks etched into the wall; another has a drawing of a giant Jesus; others have Christian crosses.

After we finish roaming D-block, we move on to the cafeteria. It's a pitch-dark room with walls decorated by out of place murals of wildlife. There are colorful, almost cheery paintings of raccoons, mountain lions, and ducks. It's nearly enough to make you forget the men who shivved each other over bites of scrambled eggs.

Next, we make our way to a large, derelict gym where prisoners once exercised. The room is dark except for the red glow of the exit sign. The rain is pouring down outside, so this is as good a place as any to stay dry while watching for the dead.

By midnight, I'm tired, and briefly consider lying down on one of the hard, metal beds in a prison cell to take a nap. But the thought of being alone with my eyes closed in that shadowy blackness makes the hair on the back of my neck bristle and my insides turn to mush. Let me tell you, I may be a bit skeptical, but I am not that skeptical.

I spend the last few hours of my night on my own, wandering D-block and the gymnasium, and observing the prison yard from a dry perch. I have second thoughts about having abandoned my companions. The darkness is so vast and unsettling you can feel it. The minutes tick by.

As my night ends, I am relieved that I haven't had an unexplained encounter. After all, what would I do if I did see a ghost? What would I do if I heard a whisper from a blackened prison cell? Or saw a shadow move out of the corner of my eye? Or looked across the yard and saw a figure standing in a window? I can promise you I would be over the fence faster than an escaping convict.

As I leave just before 4 a.m., I overhear one of my fellow paranormal investigators say he picked up someone or something growling the words "get her" when he played back one of his recordings. I don't think I need to tell you how unnerving that is. Especially for his wife. Another says he captured the indecipherable whispering of gibberish. And what sounded like a name spoken aloud.

I consider asking them to play their tapes for me. But deep down, I'm afraid I'll hear it, too.

So, I can tell you that Brushy Mountain may be haunted by ghosts. Or maybe not. But I can assure you Brushy Mountain is haunted. The abandoned prison walls are possessed by a legacy of sadness, oppression, and death so heavy and raw and cruel you can feel it deep in your bones. I feel relieved to hear the doors shut behind me as I make my way home.

KEVIN SAYLOR *was born and raised in Oak Ridge, Tennessee. He attended the University of Tennessee in Knoxville, where he studied creative writing and journalism. He spent fifteen years as a freelance columnist for the* Knoxville News Sentinel, *covering entertainment and writing the* Notsville.com *parody blog. He has written for a variety of other newspapers and magazines. His work has appeared in* Cumberland Avenue Revisited: Four Decades of Music From Knoxville Tennessee, East Tennessee Garden Stories, *and* 23 Tales: Appalachian Ghost Stories, Legends & Other Mysteries. *This was his first, and hopefully last, night spent in a maximum-security prison.*

— TWELVE —

AN EASY WAY TO GET RID OF GHOSTS
Erie, Pennsylvania

TERRY SHAW

When Deborah Lucarelli was married to her first husband back in Erie, Pennsylvania, she had to deal with unexpected houseguests. One of the visitors had an unusual sense of humor, another was annoying. A third was surprisingly helpful. The fourth? Well, that woman scared the hell out of her. It was a lot to handle.

Consider the couple's dealings with the prankster. In the early years of their marriage they rented an upstairs flat in a 100-year-old home on the west side of town. Unfortunately, the husband and wife were on different schedules. She stayed up much later than him, sitting in her rocking chair, doing homework or crafts or watching television. He rose early for shift work.

"Sometimes when he got up, he would find that solid wood rocking chair blocking his way from the bedroom," she said.

Finally, he confronted her.

"Why do you mess with me and move your chair into the dining room?" he asked.

"I can't even lift it," she answered.

And she couldn't slide the heavy piece that far, not to mention the noise it would make on the hardwood floors.

"I would never do that to the downstairs neighbors," she said.

He got white as a sheet. Then he told her it happened all the time.

Then there was the time she bought him an expensive pair of leather gloves with rabbit fur lining for Christmas. Afraid he'd lose them on a night they went out to a club, he left them on the dining room table. When they came home, one of the gloves was left atop a silver coffee pot on their buffet. The other was stuck on the faucet with the lining ripped out.

All the doors had been locked.

The downstairs neighbors hadn't heard anyone come in.

There were no footprints besides their own in the snow around the house.

Lucarelli had no clue what was going on until she visited a medium at the Lily Dale Assembly in nearby Chautauqua County, New York.

"Oh, there's an old man who once lived there," she was told. "He's in the attic and loves to scare the young man living there because he's a very nervous sort."

In the early eighties, the couple bought their first home in Millcreek, the suburb where they'd grown up. This was when things got really crazy. Lucarelli saw a ghost with her own eyes: A thin woman in a long Victorian dress would creep past their bedroom door in the middle of the night.

Lucarelli always screamed at the sight.

"My husband would turn over in bed, then tell me my eyes were closed and that I'd been dreaming," she said. "He tried to act like it was no big deal. But the thing is, I'm a very light sleeper. I can wake up if the wind blows a leaf against my window."

The guests weren't always mischievous.

Shortly after closing on their house, Lucarelli, her husband, and the real estate agent (who happened to be her sister-in-law), were discussing everything the couple needed to buy for the new place, including a lawnmower for the huge yard. The previous owner had lost her husband years earlier, and they had plenty of maintenance issues to address. But they weren't sure what they could cover.

"You two girls go get a few gallons of paint," Lucarelli's husband said. "We can afford that."

In the meantime, he had an idea. A coin collector, he sometimes came across rare finds when removing HVAC units in older homes. He would take the ducting apart to see if anything turned up.

When the women returned with the paint, they found him sitting in the empty living room, staring straight ahead at nothing, a leather wallet in front of him. It was full of cash.

"At first he couldn't talk," Lucarelli said. "But finally, after a beer, he told us what happened."

Earlier, as the women pulled out of the driveway, he abruptly got off a ladder in the basement and climbed two flights of stairs, the whole time thinking, 'Why am I doing this?' He went to an unfinished part of the attic, where he was drawn to a piece of the wall. On further inspection, he noticed a nail sticking out. He pulled it and opened a compartment in the low attic space.

"He was far too tall to stand up there, had no flashlight, and with only the light coming from the bedroom through a small opening, he reached in and pulled out the wallet."

It had five hundred dollars in cash. They had their lawnmower and more.

Later, another Lily Dale medium had a simple explanation.

"That's someone attached to the place; he once lived there and likes you both for loving his former home," the medium explained. "He sent the money because he knew you would take care of it."

Near the end of the couple's twenty-year marriage, the Victorian lady appeared again in the Millcreek house.

"This time she looked right at me and stepped into our bedroom," Lucarelli recalled. "Of course I screamed blue murder. And that time I told him, 'My eyes were wide open!'"

She knew what she saw and wasn't buying his denials any longer.

Another medium backed her up.

"Oh, you have a hitchhiking ghost who came with someone from one very old home to your new home," she said. "The spirits are there for your husband and enjoy taunting him."

That must have been true.

"After I divorced him and he moved out, I never saw her again, heard no bumps in the attic, nothing," said Lucarelli, now a resident of Myrtle Beach, South Carolina. "And I lived there until 2014."

Terry Shaw is a co-founder of Howling Hills Publishing.

— THIRTEEN —

Stalking Old Moses Wharton

Lawrence County, Pennsylvania

DOUG BROWN

My wife and I have been married thirty-two years. We met and married in Western Pennsylvania. We moved north and spent many happy years in New England but eventually returned. Our realm, Lawrence County, butts up against the state line. In just a short drive, we can see dun fields of Ohio wheat, green-gold fields of Pennsylvania corn, and an occasional field of white-flowering buckwheat.

As often as not, the workers in those fields wear the distinctive straw hats, humble broad-fall overalls with suspenders, untrimmed beards and bowl-cut coifs of the Pennsylvania Dutch. In our local Walmart, we often come across gaggles of women in modest blue dress, black cape, black bonnet, and black lace-up boots as they hunt and peck furtively through the health-and-beauty aisles. Behind the Aldi and the Arby's, it's a common sight to see their horse-and-buggies tied up. Many a night we've had the late-night silence broken by the distinctive trotting clip-clop of an Amish cart, and if you happen to peer into the cart as it passes you may lock gazes with the occupants, peering out as curiously as you might peer in, eager for some insight into the others' world.

But they're not ghosts. They don't haunt this area. They're a people alive and vital, growing crops, working construction, engaged and industrious. The superficial differences make them seem to be other, foreign, alien. I imagine we seem the same to them—distinctly other—distant, cold, wraith-like echoes of humanity they pass in the course of their bustling existence. Our conflicted cultures tell us the other is missing the point of the questions life poses.

One thing is clear: They exist in a warp in the fabric of time. They bring in crops and haul them to be milled the same way they did a hundred and fifty years ago—the same way they did two hundred and fifty years ago when they came to this country from Europe.

In a similar way, my wife and I found a similar warp in time's fabric when we returned to this borderland between the western hem of the Alleghenies and the Ohio flatlands.

In one of our favorite haunts, McConnell's Mill, you enter a timeless enclave. Commissioned as a state park in 1952 along with 2,500 surrounding acres, the area offers countless attractions of timeless natural beauty. There grassland gives way to woodland, hiding a long gorge cut by the Slippery Rock Creek—a river in all but name, with a strong current running through violent whitewater rapids. Dozens of unfortunates are known to have perished in those waters, and no doubt many more perished in similar ways prior to the state taking control. In fact, several water rescue personnel are in that number, the host that went under the waters and got pinned by the raging currents that worry the silent staring rocks. No one sees those souls, though their voices may mix with the constant crash and murmur of the frantic waters.

The park also contains several miles of hiking trails, from easy walks along the river's edge to severe climbs up the sides of the gorge. And for those who aren't satisfied with a strenuous hike, glacial boulders litter the slopes, and many climbers have fallen to serious injury or death. Eight years ago, in a sad irony, a woman perished falling from Breakneck Bridge. And yet she does not haunt this gorge.

In recent years, one hiking trail has gained fame due to its ill-fitting name: Hell's Hallow. But the name Hell's Hallow goes back to the 1850s when a lime kiln was built near the picturesque falls that now share the Hell's Hallow name. The kiln often burned days at a time, and people passing near the forge at night could see the fiery glow from the mouth of the kiln and smell the sulfurous smoke that belched forth. Hell's

Run, leading into the hollow, led through a particularly narrow branch of the gorge, and no doubt anyone passing through at night would feel the sensation of the walls closing in as the red glow of the horizon intensified and the malodorous atmosphere became more oppressive. But this is no portal to hell. The notoriety it's received in recent decades has been more a product of the internet than the netherworld.

Another falsehood is the legend of the Dark Thing, which dates back to the turn of the twenty-first century and suspiciously resembles Gollum from *The Lord of the Rings*. A few groups of school-aged kids have peddled this story, and perhaps it's gone viral. But there's nothing more old-fashioned than weaving a spine-chilling yarn as you walk your girl through a dark and eerie wood.

No, the real hauntings in McConnell's Mill State Park focus on the covered bridge (not Breakneck Bridge, but McConnell's Mill State Park Covered Bridge) and the mill itself just below the falls. This is where you might run into the souls of those who devoted the most important parts of their lives tending to the work of the mill, servicing the farmers who brought their wheat and corn and buckwheat by the wagonload slowly, carefully down the road that descended the side of the gorge. Coming from the west, folks had to navigate the sharp turn onto the covered bridge and then another sharp turn upon exiting on the other side.

Over the fifty years McConnell's Mill operated, one man's life was tied to the Mill more than any other—that of Moses

Wharton, the only custodian of Tom McConnell's Mill. Moses was born into slavery in the Carolinas. He moved with his aged mother to Western Pennsylvania where he hoped to find freedom and opportunity. Tom McConnell hired him in 1880 and he worked conscientiously until the mill closed in 1928. He walked from his cottage on the slopes of the gorge down to the mill every morning and back up the slope every evening.

Moses Wharton would sweep and clean the fourth floor of the mill where farmers would unload their corn, oats, wheat, or buckwheat. He would maintain the rollers on the third floor that ground the grain into flour, keeping them in good working order. He would clean out and keep in good repair the chutes that led down to the second floor where the product was bagged and loaded onto an outbound wagon. Tom McConnell handled the money. One or two other workers helped in the busy season. But day in and day out, for forty-eight years, Tom McConnell's mill depended on Moses Wharton. He opened up in the morning, closed down at the end of the day, and kept things running in between.

People claim to have seen him—years after the mill closed—walking to the mill in the morning, sometimes turning on the lights. Many more may have seen him and paid no mind—he just looks like he belongs there.

Others claim to see another man, an unnamed man, who also walks down to the mill in the early morning. The figure disappears into the mill and a blood-curdling scream is heard, as the troubled soul relives a tragic accident that supposedly cost him his life. But this is not Moses Wharton.

People have repeatedly reported seeing Moses by the west end of the covered bridge. He's summoned by parking your car in the middle of the bridge after dark and honking your horn. You can tell it's him by the feeling of watchful calm that comes over you as he appears to keep things moving, ushering you out of the bridge and guiding you, if you'll let him, around the tight turn at the west end of the bridge and onto the road leading up the west side of the gorge.

Another sadder soul is said to be summoned at the same spot in a similar way. When driving your car onto the covered bridge after dark, if you stop in the middle of the bridge, turn off your lights and honk three times, a sad little girl appears in your rearview mirror. We don't know the girl's name. She's clearly very shy, cowering behind the driver, fearing something she keeps reliving as she looks through the windshield. You have to wonder if Moses knows what she sees, whether he was there or regrets not being there when he might have averted tragedy.

But the bend in the road at the west end of the covered bridge—that's the best view in the park of the red board-and-batten-sided bridge with the weathered mill and the picturesque falls in the background. It's perfect for a selfie or a landscape photo. That's our favorite view. And that's where you might run into us, posing for a picture, taking a selfie, or maybe offering by gesture to take one for you. If you drive through the covered bridge, you may see us silhouetted at the western mouth of the bridge, perhaps kissing. Excuse us if we don't speak. Just know everything's OK. It'll be fine. Just don't go in the water.

DOUG BROWN *lives with his wife Susan in Grove City, Pennsylvania. His short fiction has been published in* BarBar, Half and One, *and* Solid Food Press. *His short story collection,* My Bohemian Baptism and Then Some, *was released by Serif Press. Brown's stories earned shortlist mention for the Khasi Hills Creative Prize 2023 and Globe Soup Best Short Stories 2022. He holds degrees from Carnegie Mellon and Penn State.*

— FOURTEEN —

THE KNOCKING SPIRIT
Grassy Creek, Virginia

MEGAN MCKAMEY

My ancestral roots trace back to Southwest Virginia, nestled among the rolling hills just north of Nickelsville, in the close-knit community of Grassy Creek. My great-great grandmother, Martha Isaacs, was born there in 1877, the youngest of eight children. In 1898, she married Jasper Moore.

Their small community was warm and welcoming, the kind of place where neighbors weren't just neighbors; they were kinfolk, always ready to offer a hand to those in need.

Martha and Jasper cherished a serene and tranquil life, yet their journey was not without its trials. They bore profound sorrow after losing their first two children in infancy. Nevertheless, their family grew, and they found solace in the presence of three healthy children: Mary "Ethel," George "Gaines," and my great grandmother, Lillian.

In 1918, the Spanish flu swept across the globe, leaving no corner untouched. During this pandemic, the residents of Grassy Creek banded together like never before. Neighbors checked in on one another, delivering food, medicine, and words of comfort to those confined to their beds.

As Grassy Creek continued to suffer, Jasper dedicated himself to aiding those afflicted by the flu. He was not a man of medicine, but still offered his assistance to those in need. One evening while he was away tending to a neighboring household, his wife and their two daughters fell ill with the flu.

As Martha and the girls lay bundled together in their bed, she found herself drifting in and out of a restless slumber. In the stillness of the night, a gentle tapping at the head of the bed awoke Martha. Initially dismissing it as a figment of her fevered imagination, she soon found herself wide awake as the rhythmic knocking persisted. As the last faint echoes faded into the night, a soft whisper pierced the silence, uttering the name "Charlie," the name of the little boy down the road.

Startled from her sleep, Martha sat upright in the bed, her breath catching in her throat as she struggled to make sense of the eerie encounter. In a trembling voice, she spoke into the darkness, her words hanging heavy in the air. "Little Charlie just died." This woke Ethel and Lillian from their slumber, their confusion mirroring Martha's own bewilderment as they tried to comprehend how their mother could have known this.

An hour later, the familiar creaking of the door announced Jasper's return. As he entered the bedroom, the weight of Martha's premonition still hung heavy in the air. As he approached the bed, Jasper delivered the news. "Little Charlie died about an hour ago."

The Great Depression and both World Wars brought even more hardship. Many young men, including Martha's only son, Gaines, heeded the call to serve their country. Their absence cast a shadow over Grassy Creek. Still, its people persevered.

Eventually, Gaines Moore came back to Grassy Creek. Unfortunately, his return marked the beginning of a difficult journey as he suffered with severe post-traumatic stress in the aftermath of the war.

In 1948, Jasper Moore passed away, leaving Martha alone in their home. Here, she lived the rest of her life in solitude, far from the outside world and devoid of modern amenities like a telephone. But perhaps the absence of worldly distractions allowed her to attune herself to the rhythms of the natural world and to explore the depths of her own intuition, a sixth sense, as some might call it. Or maybe the mountains harbor their own mysteries and enigmatic forces, selective in choosing those with whom they share their secrets.

As the years went by, Gaines remained haunted by his wartime experiences.

On a July morning in 1960, Martha's daughter, Lillian, and niece, Beulah, made their way to Grassy Creek to deliver tragic news. As they arrived at Martha's home, they were greeted by her as they made their way through the yard. Her eyes were filled with a haunting understanding.

Before they could mutter a word, Martha said to them, "You do not have to tell me; I already know. Gaines is dead. The Knocking Spirit visited me and called his name."

Her words hung heavy in the air. Martha's knowledge of Gaines's passing defied all rational explanation, as she had no conventional means of receiving such news. He had tragically ended his own life the day before, though some were convinced the rumors of foul play, stemming from a heated altercation in Harrogate, Tennessee, held a more sinister truth.

Martha passed in 1972, but her encounters with the Knocking Spirit live on through the generations of our family. Her home, where the Knocking Spirit made its visits, still stands to this day in eerie isolation, its cracked and peeling paint echoing a now-forgotten era. The windows, like vacant eyes, peer out into the night, reflecting only the pallor of the moon and the darkness of the surrounding woods. And within its weathered walls, there lingers the resonance of a time when the veil between the known and the unknown seemed to thin.

At the crest of the hill overlooking the house lies the Isaacs family cemetery, a silent congregation of weathered headstones. Here, Martha, Jasper, and Gaines now rest alongside those who had gone on before them. They stand as guardians over the house, their presence lingering, as if the departed souls yearn to share their stories with the living.

For now, their stories live on. And if you ever chance upon a mysterious knocking in the stillness of the night, heed the call of curiosity and listen closely. For in those hushed moments, you might find yourself in the company of The Knocking Spirit seeking to share its secrets if you dare to listen.

MEGAN MCKAMEY, *based in Kingsport, Tennessee, balances her 9-5 job with a passion for music. As a professional singer-songwriter and accomplished banjo player, she's graced stages nationwide, including the renowned "Hatfield and McCoy Dinner Show" in Pigeon Forge. Megan's roots in the Appalachian Mountains deeply influence her artistry. She wrote this generational tale, passed down from her late grandmother, to honor her family and preserve the storytelling traditions of her upbringing.*

— FIFTEEN —

SEVENTH SON
Appalachia, Virginia

MATT HOPKINS

My grandfather, Dewey Williams, was the seventh son of a seventh son. Everyone swore this gave him unique powers and abilities. I would argue this was just superstition if I hadn't witnessed several things in his presence and at the time of his death.

He once cured a baby of thrush, simply by blowing in his mouth.

I saw him coax wild deer to him in the woods.

He would soothe people who were in severe pain, giving the doctor time to care for them.

This is a story he told me one afternoon after he got onto me for trying to dig a foxhole in his freshly plowed garden. It took place during WWI in the mountains of Southwest Virginia, not far from the Kentucky border. My grandfather was too young to fight at the time, though several of his brothers served. Grandpa started working in the mines to help support the family and the farm. He walked several miles back and forth to work every day along trails that still carried wagon and foot traffic through heavily wooded areas.

"This was 'afore they built roads everywhere and a person could walk for days, just enjoying what God gave us," he liked to say.

One early spring evening, he had just finished his shift and the sun was starting to slowly slip behind the mountain. There would be just enough daylight left for him to feed the hogs. Then he could have what dinner his momma had left out for him on the stove.

He hoped it was fried chicken, though his family usually didn't have that until Sunday. It was a special treat for having to trudge to the church and listen to Parson Jones' sermon. Mama had promised Papa years ago that she would always make fried chicken on Sunday, if he could stay awake and not snore through the sermon. Dewey smiled to himself, remembering all the times he and his brothers poked and prodded their dad to make sure he didn't fall asleep.

His smile and feeling faded as he remembered his brothers. Two were in the war in France. His brother Benjamin had written him a letter from over there. Benjamin sailed on a big ship for almost a week to get there. That was after a day-and-a-half train ride here in the U.S. There were even several days marching once they got off the boat. This was to just get to the place where they were supposed to fight the Germans. They called them Huns instead of Germans. Dewey wasn't sure why they called them that. It seemed more like a romantic term for lovers.

Thinking of France and the Germans made him miss his brothers. The family received a letter at least once a month. Isaiah had only written twice since making it there. Each letter told how well the boys were doing. They both would be home soon. The Huns couldn't handle the likes of them. The only complaint was the food. They couldn't wait to get home and have Ma's great cooking.

Dewey was lost in thought about his brothers and the dinner waiting for him. He walked down the last steep curvy section in the road just before getting home. He heard a rumble that jerked him out of his thoughts. No way it was thunder! The sky was clear. However, the rumbling did not stop. It seemed to increase and get closer. Dewey looked about trying to pin-point where the noise was coming from. He swung around to face the way he had just come. That's when he saw a loaded wagon coming down the mountain toward him.

That was weird to see this late in the day. The road was narrow and treacherous in good light. Most teamsters would be afraid to get caught in the dark. A horse could misstep. That could cause the whole rig to go over the edge. There were spots where the wagoner, horses, and wagon could easily plunge fifty feet or more over the side.

The sound came closer.

Dewey looked for a place to get off the trail. He wasn't in the best of spots. To his left the bank went up a good fifteen feet. No way for him to climb that. The right was a steep drop-off. There was a little area where a spring came out on the left a bit farther down the road. Dewey decided to run for it.

When he glanced over his shoulder, nothing could have prepared him for what was coming his way. The sight almost made him stumble and fall. His heart seemed to stop beating, frozen in fear. He gasped several times trying to fill his lungs with air. When his breath finally came, it seemed much colder than it should have been.

A funeral wagon bore down upon him. Two dark gray horses were tethered in the lead. What seemed like smoke encircled their heads with each labored breath. Their hooves clattered as if on stone, although they traveled a dirt trail. A dark figure sat in the seat. A cloth was pulled up over his nose. A dark hat with a red feather was pulled down to his brow. Only his eyes were visible as he drove the wagon forward. His long whip snapped above the horses' heads, urging them to move ever forward.

A black hearse was uncommon in the mountains. The only time Dewey had seen one was when the wife of a mine superintendent had died down in town. This one was not shiny and pristine. The cloth that covered the viewing window was tattered and flapped through holes where glass should have been. The wood was dull, dusty, and chipped. It had the look of barn lumber filled with worm rot.

The hearse should not have been able to move, let alone travel the mountain roads. The driver did not whip the animals so they overtook him. The dark figure kept them at a pace that made Dewey run forward at a light pace he could manage easily. There was no push to rush him down the trail. The wagon did not seem to be trying to crush his form under the creaking wheels. There was only the sensation that he was being pushed forward. There was a place it wanted him to go.

Dewey stopped and yelled back at the dark driver. "What do you want from me?"

Silence and the crack of the whip was the reply. The hearse came closer at the same pace. Not speeding up or slowing down. Dewey began to calculate things in his mind. It was only three quarters of a mile to the area where there was the hollow for the spring. It was probably another half of a mile to his home from there. His home would be the safest place for him. However, a part of him was afraid of what might happen to his parents or his sister. This thing could not go near them. He had heard tales of demons driving dark coaches or riding dark horses through the mountains since he was young.

He focused on running at a steady pace. There was no pain as he ran. The fear had taken that away. Dewey knew he had to get to the alcove. His mind raced with terrible thoughts.

Was this a demon come to take him to hell? Was it his time to die? Was this a test by God to see if he was worthy?

His mind was so occupied he almost missed the alcove with the spring. At the last second, he threw his whole body to the left. It was only five feet deep, but Dewey scrambled to the very back to be safe from the driver and hearse. His heart thundered in his ears, as he heard the horses slow to a walk. The creaking of the wheels slowed as well. He could hear the creaking of the leather reins when the wagon stopped in front of where he crouched.

Dewey did not want to look, but he made himself. He stared straight into the eyes of the coachman. They were icy blue. Coldness crept into Dewey, like he would never be warm again. The coachman gestured to the back of the hearse with his head. He had to do it several more times before Dewey started to slowly shift to look.

It took everything in him to slowly turn his head to where the specter gestured. Dewey expected to see an empty coffin waiting for him. But the compartment was not empty. There was a body already in it. Slowly he crept forward trying to see who was there. He was almost out of the alcove when he realized the body was wearing an Army uniform. Dewey screamed as he tried to lurch forward to see the face. A scrap of the curtain kept blowing in the way.

Before Dewey could reach the hearse, the coachmen yelled and snapped the whip. The horses took off. This time they sprinted down the road. Dewey yelled in rage and pain. He sprinted after the dark wagon. It was no good. It pulled far ahead of him until it was out of sight, just around the bend before his house. He kept running as fast as he could. He needed to tell his family what he saw. His Pa would know what to do. There had to be some way to stop whatever was happening.

All thoughts dropped out of his head as he ran into his yard. The parson was standing on the porch talking to his father. His mother and sister were clutching each other. They went between screaming and crying as he approached.

Dewey had to take several quick breaths. "Pa?"

His father looked at him with tears in his eyes. The old man couldn't speak.

It was Parson Jones who handed him a piece of paper.

"I am sorry, boy," he said softly. "You brother Benjamin was a good man. If it makes you feel any better, that letter says he died a hero."

MATT HOPKINS *was the last person born in the doctor's office in Appalachia, Virginia. His father was a coal miner, and his mother was a nurse. He grew up in Big Stone Gap, attended Clinch Valley College, and joined the Virginia National Guard, retiring in 2021. He and his wife Denora have three daughters and live in Johnson City, Tennessee. When not spending time with his family, he's reading, writing, or riding motorcycles.*

— SIXTEEN —

EDDIE'S APPARITION
Knoxville, Tennessee

SHERI MCCARTER

Weekend stays at my grandmother's house meant sweaty backyard games of tag, Mayfield's Neapolitan ice cream melting in a cone, possibly a late-night movie. But for my twin brother and and me, the absolute pinnacle of evening activities was a séance, and my grandmother wouldn't disappoint. The three of us would pull our chairs up close to the small kitchen table, candle flickering brightly in the center of the lace tablecloth. We would clasp our hands together with hers to strengthen our circle. With the fragrance of honeysuckle and freshly mown grass wafting through the curtains, she would whip us into a giggling, eight-year-old frenzy calling out for any spirits in the room to speak to us and then answering back in wailing tones of restless agony.

"Whooo is with us? It's getting cold in here. I know you're with us. Tell us your *name*," she intoned as she clutched our hands tighter.

"Mariah," the high, thin voice woefully replied. "I'm sooo *cold*."

"Mariah! Are you in pain? Give us a sign!"

At the height of contact with whatever spirit she had summoned, with our wide eyes and mouths forming identical Os, she would bang the underside of the table, sending us into shrieks of terror and delight. Every single time. It never got old, and I don't think we ever stopped halfway believing it just might be real.

Edna Maria O'Hanlon Buckner, who only ever went by Eddie, was feisty, full of humor, adventure, and the not-so-occasional dirty joke, which was immediately followed by "God forgive me. I'm going to have to get right soon. I won't live forever."

As kids, we loved spending the weekend with her, and she would tell us wild stories of her youth in Manchester. Trading her lunch money for cigarettes (fags in her vernacular) and going to dances with her group of raucous girlfriends. Invariably, we begged her to tell the story of the neighborhood pie man who pushed his rolling cart through the streets and alleyways selling delicious meat pies. It was only when the neighborhood cats started disappearing that his customers caught on to the main ingredient. Was this a true tale or one she read in a Penny Dreadful growing up in England? It's hard to say; she did love a fantastic tale, evidenced by the stack of National Enquirer and The Sun magazines, which she always referred to as her "papers," piled high by her reading chair.

Eddie was comfortable with the supernatural, as likely to tell me about a cake dish mysteriously flying off the top of the refrigerator and crashing to the floor as she was to talk about a cake she planned to bake. I believe for many of her generation the veil between the living and the dead was thinner.

A WWII veteran, she met and married my grandfather while they were both serving overseas. He had deep Appalachian roots, and I recall how on an evening walk with him a black cat crossed the road ahead of us and we had to double back to take a different path home. He worked nightshift and slept much of the day but regaled us with the story of his missing hand, which he lost while working on a piece of machinery that someone carelessly switched on. Meanwhile, my grandmother worked for a local furniture manufacturer and told stories of coworkers losing fingers that would later turn up in someone's lunch box.

They lived in North Knoxville on the edge of Happy Hollow, an area which has become trendy in the last decade but was scruffy as an alley cat in the 1980s. Like most kids of that decade, my brother and I had dawn-to-dusk free reign of the neighborhood, so we knew most of the neighbors. Two of our favorites, Ann and Jim Gainor, lived nearby in a small house with a neat little yard. Ann would invite us into the kitchen for popsicles on the hottest of days, and Jim would let us walk with him to inspect his miniature garden out back in the cool of the evening. They were steadfast friends of my grandparents, and when my grandfather passed, they looked out for my grandmother. She looked out for them in return.

As my brother and I crossed the threshold from childhood to adolescence and became more independent, our weekend excursions to my grandmother's house became less frequent. We still visited along with our parents, but we didn't stay overnight, and the seances and backyard games were relegated to the land of childhood lore.

Jim and Ann grew older too, and Jim's health began to decline. Along with physical ailments, Jim began to show signs of dementia. He would sometimes hallucinate, and Ann would share her concerns with my grandmother, who had seen for herself first-hand during visits. Ann and Jim were chosen family, and it was hard for my grandmother to witness the toll that illness took on him. Jim had a smile that took up serious real estate on his face. His tanned skin stretched around it to accommodate its magnitude, and the skin crinkled around his sparkling blue eyes. Watching that smile fade was a sad affair. Seeing the fear that had crept into those sparkling eyes was heart-breaking.

Another balmy summer day, I listened to my grandmother's measured voice on the phone. It was full of Appalachia but never quite lost the lilt of her Manchester accent. "I had a visit from Jim Gainor last night." She sounded solemn. "He came into my room and sat down on the edge of my bed. He was in his pajamas, pale blue with a darker blue stripe."

This had taken an odd turn, and I worried he was wandering out in the night in the middle of one of his increasingly frequent episodes. I resisted the urge to chide her for leaving her door unlocked, waiting for the right moment to discuss it without interrupting her story.

"He told me not to be sad," she continued, "but it was time for him go. He thanked me for our friendship and asked me to look after Ann."

"That sounds like a very vivid dream," I replied cautiously.

"Oh, it wasn't a dream. He was as real and solid as you, and he was there sitting casually on the side of my bed. I knew he was there, but I also knew he wasn't alive. He spoke to me quietly, reassuring me that he felt whole again, happy, and I shouldn't be sad or afraid. When he got up to go, I could feel the weight of him leaving my bed. It was peaceful, and I must have fallen back asleep because when I woke up again it was to the sound of the phone ringing."

I felt a chill creeping up the back of my neck and asked the inevitable question. "Who called?"

"It was Ann asking for my help, telling me that Jim had passed during the night," she answered. "I pulled on my clothes and walked over to her house. The sun was just coming up. When I got there, Jim was lying in bed, peacefully, wearing the same pajamas he had visited me in during the night."

For years, I wondered over that story, and I still do wonder. What I can tell you is my grandmother passed twenty years ago when my first-born daughter was only three months old. She loved my daughter, and I am so happy she had the chance to meet her and hold her. My daughter's stormy-sea-colored eyes that would eventually settle into a shade of blue green so like my grandmother's locked into a gaze with her. Both were mesmerized.

In the week following my grandmother's passing, as I sat holding my infant daughter in my comfortable, overstuffed corner chair, she was fond of gazing over my shoulder, smiling and cooing with delight at absolutely nothing I could see. Again, she was mesmerized, and no amount of cajoling could divert her attention back to me. Tears swam, making my vision watery, and then overflowed, landing in fat drops on my daughter's fluffy onesie. Sometimes the veil between the living and the dead is thinner.

SHERI MCCARTER *is an educator who lives in Maryville, Tennessee, and enjoys researching and writing about early American history. She presents regularly on the Battle of Kings Mountain and will do so in period costume when the mood strikes. When not teaching, Sheri is busy organizing events, facilitating her writers' group, and participating in various initiatives as Blount County Public Library's writer-in-residence. She enjoys spending time with her daughters, reading with her dog on her lap, theater, cooking, and all things avian.*

Nº —SEVENTEEN—

LONG GONE LONESOME BLUES
Knoxville, Tennessee

LAURA STILL

Sometimes when you start telling a story, you don't know all of it. Since I began researching and sharing Knoxville's ghostly history, new pieces of stories keep finding their way to me, maybe because people need a sympathetic listener who won't scoff at their experience, or they want to add more evidence to the tale. Whatever the reason, I'm always honored, even when the sources prefer to remain anonymous for professional reasons. Luckily, my profession involves finding and retelling weird things people might not believe—like the haunting of the Andrew Johnson building.

Built in 1928, the Andrew Johnson was once the tallest building in Tennessee. It's still there, on the northeast corner of Gay Street and Hill Avenue. The luxury hotel hosted wealthy travelers to the Smokies and well-heeled locals who enjoyed its swanky restaurant featuring an elegant organist playing popular classics. In the 1930s, the penthouse welcomed a much livelier clientèle as the broadcast home of WNOX radio's Mid-Day Merry-Go-Round. After the hotel closed, the building rented office space to various businesses, including Whittle Communications, before becoming the headquarters of Knox County Schools. So for many years the brick edifice, loomed over by modern glass skyscrapers to its north, shut down at night and its lights went dim. The marble-floored hallways were rumored to be not quite silent, for there were illusive traces of past visitors, guests who left never to return.

The hotel, considered the best in town in its glory days, was the first choice of many visiting celebrities. In 1936, pioneer female aviator Amelia Earhart checked in for a brief visit and consented to an interview for the local paper. She told the reporter she didn't expect to die of old age; flying was a perilous business. She disappeared a year later, her plane lost somewhere in the Pacific. The celebrated Russian composer Sergei Rachmaninoff spent the night in the Andrew Johnson in 1943 after giving a concert at the University of Tennessee Alumni Gym. It was his final performance. Intense pain caused him to cancel the rest of his tour, and he died of cancer three months later. Knoxville and the Andrew Johnson developed a reputation as a last stop.

One guest who checked into the hotel may have never checked out. On New Year's Eve 1952, teenage chauffeur Charles Carr requested a room for himself and his employer, country music star Hank Williams. The singer-songwriter who changed country music forever was only passing through; he had booked a flight from Knoxville to Charleston, West Virginia, the next stop on his concert tour. Bad weather canceled the flight, and it was 6:08 p.m. by the time he and Carr got to their room. Williams, by some reports, needed assistance to get there, and rumors persist he had visited a local doctor for a shot of morphine and a prescription before his arrival.

Earlier in the year, the twenty-nine-year-old Williams had been diagnosed with acute alcoholism and a painful back injury had caused him to become addicted to painkillers. Carr ordered two steak dinners from room service a little later, but Williams didn't eat much. He began to hiccup and go into convulsions afterward and the hotel called Dr. Paul Cardwell from his Cumberland Avenue office, three blocks away. Dr. Cardwell would testify Williams was inebriated and that he saw pills in the room, but the medicine bottle sat unopened. The doctor needed to get the convulsions under control so he gave Williams an injection of morphine and another of vitamin B12. He had the patient lie down on his hotel bed and waited till Williams went to sleep before leaving.

At 10:45 p.m. Carr called the front desk to check out, saying "they had decided" to get an early start to West

Virginia, but he would need some help getting his boss to the car. Hank was so deeply unconscious he had rolled out of bed to the floor without waking. Porters and doormen carried him through the hotel and loaded him into the car, a baby-blue 1952 Cadillac. The helpers described Williams as unresponsive, cool to the touch, and silent except for a coughing noise as they propped him up in the back seat.

For over 60 years doctors, investigators, and witnesses have argued about whether the sound could have been a death rattle. The senior investigator in charge of the inquiry into the singer's death concluded from the amount of medication Hank had in his system that Williams most likely died in the hotel. The family accepted his conclusion, but conflicting testimony from Carr and others has kept the controversy alive to this day. The death of Hank Williams is shrouded in mystery as dark as the deserted corridors of the Andrew Johnson after closing. Dark, but perhaps not quite empty.

Numerous anecdotes from maintenance and cleaning staff tell of inexplicable voices, disembodied and strange, heard on floors where no one should be, on the other side of locked doors. On rare occasions, and especially around New Year's Eve, faint and far-off, someone can be heard singing, accompanied by the strumming of a guitar.

A lady who worked in the building several years ago told me she came in on New Year's Day once and was teased by the maintenance man who let her in for working when everyone else was home watching football. After she had worked a couple of hours, she began to hear footsteps pacing the floor above her, and snatches of song. She went to the maintenance office to tell the man she was leaving and mentioned what she heard. He insisted no one else had entered, and they went up to the floor to check. It was dark and deserted, and when he opened the office above hers, it was empty. Listening to the radio on the way home she tuned to a country station and suddenly recognized the song she'd heard. Jambalaya was getting a lot of airplay on radio stations in 1952 ... it appeared Hank still likes to practice singing it. She stayed home on New Year's after that.

Recently, a group of developers bought the Andrew Johnson building. They plan to reopen it as a boutique hotel with rental apartments available in part of the building. The renovations have continued start-stop for over a year now, somewhat behind the original schedule for various reasons: the supply issues and increased costs due to the pandemic, labor shortages in the construction industry, and so on. The corridors are mostly deserted both night and day now. Or maybe not, according to one of the maintenance team I had as a guest on a tour one night.

After the tour, he asked to talk to me about the Andrew Johnson. A couple of months before, he had rushed to the building in the middle of the night when frozen pipes caused a major water leak. Plumbers showed up to handle the emergency, and after they had stopped the immediate problem, he had to inspect all the floors to make sure the faucets were turned off, toilets were not running, and water wasn't seeping anywhere.

He began working systematically through all the floors and on one of the upper floors entered a men's restroom near the elevator to check the sinks. Everything was fine, but as he started to open the door back to the hallway, he heard heavy, dragging footsteps on the other side. As he was the only person authorized to be in the upper part of the building, he knew he should go out and find out what was happening, but he froze, hand on the doorknob and heart thudding. He forced himself to pull open the door.

He saw no one when he stepped into the corridor, but he could still hear the weighted footsteps, and as they drew level with him, there was a slight thud and muted exclamation, as if someone had lost their grip on what—or who—they were carrying. He felt something brush against his arm, and then the footfalls resumed, fading away into the darkness. The elevator was just around that corner, but he turned and ran for the stairs.

After he finished the story, I remembered the only cold spell we'd had the previous winter had been during the holidays, between Christmas and New Year's. He told me what floor, but to keep his employers happy he swore me to secrecy. However, if you happen to make reservations after the new Andrew Johnson hotel opens, my advice is that you might sleep better on a lower floor.

LAURA STILL *is a poet, playwright, and author. She created Knoxville Walking Tours in 2012 and works full-time as a storyteller and walking history guide. She has researched and written fifteen tours, including three ghost walks. She partners with the Knoxville History Project and proceeds from her tours support it and other history-oriented Knoxville nonprofits. Co-owner of Celtic Cat Publishing since 2016, she has written four books:* Guardians (2009), Acts of the Apostles, Vol. I, (2010), A Haunted History of Knoxville (2014), *and* A Fair Shake: The Leaders of the Fight for Women's Rights in Knoxville (2021).

— EIGHTEEN —

A HAUNTED HOMEPLACE
Scott County, Virginia

JESSICA FISCHER

In the South, old homeplaces are a reminder of the ties that bind us to those who share our bloodline, history, and heritage. They provide a sense of belonging and comfort. They're also where some of our fondest memories are made—from Sunday suppers around a well-worn dinner table to holiday gatherings where laughter and stories echo through the halls.

But growing up, Mariah Cole always felt a little uneasy when visiting the two-story white farmhouse that had been in her family for more than 200 years.

Mariah's ancestor, Abraham Fulkerson, was born in Somerset County, New Jersey, and later moved to North Carolina. He settled in Scott County, Virginia, after serving in the Battle of King's Mountain during the Revolutionary War. In 1783, he built his growing family a two-story hand-hewn log home in Little Valley, just a stone's throw from the banks of the North Fork of the Holston River near what's now the Hiltons community.

Generations of Fulkerson's descendants lived—and died—in the old homeplace, evidenced by the small cemetery behind the house, where a few gravestones are still visible if you know just where to look.

As the farmstead passed from one generation to the next, so, too, did tales of strange sights and sounds inside the home's weathered walls.

Mariah's great-grandmother, Jesse Hilton Addington, who bought the house with her husband Ezra in 1921, recounted once hearing what sounded like a barrel of walnuts spill and roll across the second story's uneven plank floor. When she climbed the narrow set of stairs to the low-ceilinged loft to investigate, she found no walnuts and nothing out of place.

Mariah had plenty of her own encounters with the home's mysterious mischief-makers, whomever or whatever they might be.

While in college, she and a friend were walking in the front yard and saw what appeared to be a young boy around four or five years old with sandy brown hair and a sad look on his face peering out a ground-floor window. That same friend was also with her upstairs in the house one afternoon when they heard the distinct sound of footsteps that started in the kitchen, passed through the dining room and stopped at the foot of the staircase. Mariah thought her grandmother had walked over from her own home next door to say hello, but when the two girls went downstairs to greet her, no one was there.

Years later, Mariah and her husband renovated the house, adding a bedroom and modern kitchen and bath off the back before moving in with their two dogs. The dogs would often sit in the living room staring at someone or something their humans' eyes couldn't see, but otherwise, nothing much out of the ordinary happened—at first. Shortly after their son was born, however, the home's supernatural squatters seemed to grow more restless—or at least a touch more mischievous.

Their son's toys would often light up and sound off on their own. On multiple occasions, the Coles would awaken to find that overnight, two framed photos sitting atop a piano in the living room had been turned to face the wall.

One night, shortly after their son had dozed off in his crib in the downstairs nursery, movement on the video baby monitor caught Mariah's attention. She and her husband, Matt, watched as what looked like a young child's arm, then head, moved across the screen.

"The next day I went into our son's room and said, 'Whoever is here, you can stay, but please leave our son alone.' I never saw or heard anything on the baby monitor after that, although the photos on the piano would still move."

A couple of years later, the Coles moved to Mariah's late

grandmother's house next door, although Matt kept his office and continued to work from home in the old Fulkerson-Hilton house. One night, Mariah walked across the yard to the old house to do some cleaning.

Shortly after she stepped through the back door, she sensed someone watching her.

"The feeling was so strong it made the hairs on the back of my neck stand up," she remembers. "I looked around, and of course no one was there. I called out to the house saying, 'I know I haven't been out here in a while, but it's just me, and I'm doing some cleaning.' Immediately, the feeling of being watched went away. I never felt that way again."

Eventually, Mariah's family sold the Fulkerson-Hilton House, now on the National Register of Historic Places, to some long-time family friends, who have since turned it into a vacation rental property. The extra foot traffic seemed to stir up the home's haints.

One winter night, Rebecca Arrington, who now owns the place with her husband, Jeff, stopped by with her dog Lucy. Sitting on the couch in the living room enjoying a fire in the original hand-chiseled stone fireplace, Rebecca nearly jumped out of her skin when she heard the unmistakable sound of a glass marble hit the wooden floor above her head and roll from one side of the second story floor to the other. Little Lucy was terrified, too.

They both ran as fast as their legs would carry them to her brother-in-law's house next door. He returned with Rebecca, and they both searched the second floor from top to bottom for the source of the sound. No marble—or anything else that could have accounted for such a sound—was found.

Nor could the Arringtons pinpoint what kept activating the motion sensors around the house. Once, the motion sensor in the living room alerted them to activity, but when they checked the monitor, nothing was there—although they could hear two women talking in the kitchen. Rebecca remembers hearing one of them ask the other, "Do you think there will be enough?"

Even guests have reported strange encounters. A woman whose family spent a week in the house emailed the Arringtons after their visit to ask if anyone named Sylvia had ever lived in the home. One of her daughters, who was sleeping in the bunk room that the Coles had previously used as a nursery, said she'd dreamed that a woman named Sylvia was in the room with her. Sylvia told her that she used to care for children in the house.

A couple of nights later, the woman, who was sleeping in the upstairs loft, awoke from a nightmare to the distinct feeling of someone sitting at the foot of her bed. She wasn't scared of this unseen being, which she believed to be a woman—rather, she felt comforted by her presence. So it seems as if the otherworldly inhabitants of the Fulkerson-Hilton house have every intention of sticking around. And as long as they remain hospitable haunts, the Arringtons say that's just fine.

JESSICA FISCHER *knows a thing or two about tale-telling. She spent the first two decades of her career as a newspaper reporter and editor and now works in public relations, crafting and sharing stories in a corporate setting. Jessica lives on her family's farm in Hiltons, Virginia, with her husband, children, granddaughter and a trio of furry, four-legged companions. When she isn't writing, you'll probably find her camping, reading, crafting, or performing with her church's puppet troupe.*

— NINETEEN —

BELKIS SALON AND SPA AND SPIRITS

Newland, North Carolina

RAINA WISEMAN

Belkis Benavides owns a nail salon in Newland, North Carolina, with two pedicure chairs, one employee, and three ghosts.

It's not her first experience with the supernatural. Born in the Dominican Republic, Belkis first felt the presence of ghosts when she was eight years old.

"I've always felt things that weren't normal," she said.

When Belkis was a little girl, she saw the devil—a big, monstrous-looking man with red eyes. To this day, she prays to God that she'll never see him again.

She was haunted by her first boyfriend, too. A few years after their breakup, he died in surgery. When living with her first husband in Puerto Rico, she began seeing the ex-boyfriend on the foot of her bed. Her husband went to a woman who practiced voodoo for help. He was told to take twenty-one pennies to a cemetery as an offering.

Belkis never saw her ex-boyfriend after that.

Belkis Salon and Spa is in the heart of Newland, the Avery County seat with a population of just over 700. It's on the corner of one of the town's two traffic lights. The whole block, including a funeral home, was destroyed by fire in 1941. The rebuilt structure has been home to various businesses, including a pharmacy, flower shop, and diner. Today, it's the salon and a Mexican restaurant.

Nothing about the bright and inviting place would make you think it's haunted. Belkis has plenty of welcoming decorations, including a very large Christmas village in the winter and flowers every spring and summer. But right after she bought it in 2005, she felt the presence of more than her clients.

Belkis Salon and Spa is on the ground level of the building with basement storage. More than once, after she's closed for the day and locked up, Belkis has been downstairs and heard someone walking across her shop floor above. Every time, no one is there. Once she heard footsteps and returned to find muddy shoe prints in her front room, even though the door had been locked.

She's only felt and heard the ghosts—never saw them. That doesn't mean she likes her supernatural residents.

"I don't feel scared in the salon anymore, except when I'm downstairs," she said. "Sometimes I can feel somebody looking at me or feel someone behind me down there. For a while I wouldn't go down there by myself."

She did sprinkle holy water and burn incense once and thinks the shop has felt more peaceful ever since.

After nearly 20 years in business, only two clients have mentioned her ghosts.

Around 2010, a thirteen-year-old boy was sitting in a corner chair while his mother got a manicure. Suddenly, he looked up and addressed Belkis.

"Do you know you have ghosts downstairs?"

"How do you know?" Belkis asked, curious because she hadn't mentioned anything to him or his mom. And he'd never been downstairs.

"You have three," he said. "Two are good. One is bad."

Then he went back to whatever he was doing to pass the time.

Besides that, a regular client has mentioned feeling ghosts during her appointments. She even saw some of Belkis' decorative vines move and said it was the ghost of an old friend.

Belkis doesn't know any of the ghosts or their stories but did have an unusual experience after a beloved client suddenly passed away in 2018. That was a Thursday, and the client had an appointment on Saturday with Belkis' niece. When the time came, Belkis felt wind blow the shop's front door open and knew it was the woman coming to her appointment from the beyond.

Today, she's tired of her supernatural connection.

"I don't like it," she said. "I don't like to be by myself because I know I'm going to hear something. Sometimes I feel scared when it's too close to me. I don't want to see any more in my life. You don't want to see things that don't belong to this world."

RAINA WISEMAN *grew up in Altamont, North Carolina, and now lives in Johnson City, Tennessee. She's an alumna of East Tennessee State University's Brand and Media Strategy graduate program and has worked in corporate and higher education marketing. In her free time, she explores local eats and treats through her food Instagram @easttenneats.*

— TWENTY —

THE SWINGING GATE OF FERN LAKE HOLLOW

Middlesboro, Kentucky

LARRY D. THACKER

This is an old family story about the author's grandfathers and a great uncle.

A blur of darkness crept over Middlesboro. There was something about this time of evening. The dangerous gloaming. The Little Las Vegas of the Central Appalachian coalfields brimmed with vibrancy, its infamous activity flavored with the underlying edginess so common in wide-open towns infected with the side effects of prohibition.

The busiest spot centered along Cumberland Avenue and 19th Street, a crowded intersection a single block east of Fountain Square, where laughter and music pulsed through the streets almost as loudly as the Model T Fords and Hupmobiles scooting along in search of closer parking to card games and saloons. Enticing coos of prostitutes laced the noise.

A Christian band marched its way across the street, heading west on Cumberland, straining against the block's sinful racket, the chorus singing hymns against the hellbound wreck surrounding them. The sounds of night mixed along the streets and flowed into open windows. Horse hooves and buggy wheels atop uneven cobbled roads, the constant chatters and chings of silver and china. It was business as usual on a Friday night. The isolated coal town overflowed with out-of-towners. The height of prohibition in effect, men and woman drunk out of their minds on moonshine and whiskey. Everyone apparently happy, but someone bound to die. A typical Middlesboro weekend in Southeast Kentucky. Maybe this weekend would be different. Maybe no one would end up a headline come Monday morning's paper.

Peering out a front room window, squinting through the quickening twilight blanketing the southern side of town, Walter pulled his watch from his trouser pocket and glanced at the time.

"I'm gonna be late," he mumbled under his breath. "They'd better wait on me."

The sun was racing down around his family's Lake Hill home. Walter suspected it would be nearly dark by the time he managed to get to Howard and Johnny's place, after which they'd make their usual weekend rounds down Fern Lake Hollow toward Mud Lick. He didn't particularly like walking the tracks in pitch dark, especially on cloudy, moonless nights like this one promised. He knew that, especially after dark, the tracks—though quick and easy across Southside—were where teenagers went to find trouble. Everyone knew trouble was always right around the bend.

Walter's mother called to him.

"You finished up them chores?"

"Yes'm," his fading voice yelled back. "Gonna see Howard and Johnny now. I'll be back late!" He was already down the steps off the front porch with a jump, around their small home, and across the yard by the time he'd finished his reply.

If Walter was lucky, the other fellas, brothers who lived a mile off into Fern Lake Hollow, would be already waiting on the tracks near the halfway point. Like every other teenage boy in town, he looked forward to slipping away with his buddies and "runnin' round" as soon as he could get free. Friday and Saturday nights seemed like the only time to go socializing, when school and chores weren't interfering.

His lanky limbs propelled him into the dusk and he was at the meeting point in no time. Howard and Johnny were there along the south side of the tracks, standing on the bank. Walter barely made out their shapes in the failing light, but he heard them.

"Where you been?" one yelled.

"Chores," he mumbled back in a half whisper. Sounds carried in a strange echo down the tracks, like over water. "You waitin' long?" he asked, finally making out their faces. He took a small, unassuming bottle of clear liquid from his left coat pocket and handed it to Johnny.

"Naw. Just finished ours, too," Johnny said, taking a swig from the bottle and grimacing before handing it back.

"Let's get a move on," Walter said. "It's about too dark to see."

The boys were excited and commenced their usual leisurely, but watchful pace westward along the tracks. Keeping a sharp eye and ear out for trains approaching from around the bend or from behind, they went along, their footsteps lit from dim lamps in houses occasionally lining both sides of the tracks. They'd grow quieter as they passed these little houses, knowing their business was theirs, and people in the houses weren't keen to anyone walking the tracks.

For a while, Lake Hill towered eerily silent and dark to their left, in sharp contrast to the noise and hovering glow of the sky over town ahead and to their right. From time to time they'd hear an outburst of heavy laughter from downtown or a card game up on the hill or farther into the hollow. Sound traveled strangely. You could never tell where something really was in the dark.

After some minutes, Howard called for the other two to hold up. They stopped and watched as Howard knelt down, placing both hands and his left ear on a cool rail.

Puzzled, Johnny asked, "Whatcha doin' that for?"

"Shhh!" Howard hissed. "Listenin' for trains. Iffen ya listen real close, sometimes you can hear if they's a train…" Howard stopped speaking abruptly and stood, straining to see in the direction they were headed. Howard was the oldest of the three, though still a teenager, and liked to play big brother. "Y'all hear that?" he asked.

"Hear what?" Walter asked, jerking his head around expecting to see the lights of a train round the tracks ahead.

"I heard a shout."

"Where 'bouts?" Johnny asked, listening closer.

They stood motionless on the tracks waiting for the sound to repeat. A few seconds later, the other two heard something in the distance as well; short bursts of anger and the creak and slam of a screen door echoing toward them.

Howard pointed down the tracks. "There it is!"

They all heard it, angry screams and shouts, from what sounded like a fight.

Howard whispered, "Let's go," but the other two were already making their way swiftly and quietly toward the ruckus.

Their torsos bent forward at the waist to get as low as possible, they hurried along cautiously. After another hundred yards, they veered left into a deep ditch. Well hidden, they continued creeping, close to the ground. Listening as the trouble got louder.

Soon they were close enough to see some of the commotion. Taking their cue from Walter, who counted to three under his breath, they raised their heads over the berm's edge in unison, spying through tall grass at a dimly lit house a stone's throw away on the north side of the tracks.

Through the darkness, lit faintly by the windows of the shotgun shack, they saw a tall, gangly man in a black three-piece suit and fedora standing by the gate in the front yard. They saw another man in shirt sleeves staggering and screaming obscenities from the front porch. Both were obviously intoxicated, their voices slurred, their steps unsteady. Pointing at each other, screaming threats back and forth, and exchanging gestures the boys couldn't make out. The men seemed to have already been in a scuffle. Their clothes were ruffled and torn. Blood stained their white shirts. The one man's tie was undone and hanging.

As their eyes adjusted the boys observed the unfolding scene, mesmerized by such unexpected excitement. Howard noticed the tall man at the gate fumbling with something he'd pulled from his coat pocket. It was a pistol and he motioned for the others to be still. In another second the man on the porch produced his own pistol.

The men were drawing down on each other right before the boys' eyes. Filled with excitement and terror, they braced themselves against the bank, wanting to duck yet forcing themselves to watch. Curiosity was too strong.

The men drew their weapons in unison, still shouting at the top of their lungs, cursing each other. It felt like slow motion. Two shots rang out.

The man on the porch crashed violently backward through the doorway of the house into the front room, glass shattering and screen tangling around his body. The other man lurched and collapsed heavily across the gate in front of him. With that impact of the man's weight, the gate swung open with a burdened groan.

Both men lay still. All the boys could hear were the barking of the neighborhood dogs, their own hearts thumping in their ears, and a lady scream from within the house.

"Oh, Lordy! Murder! Murder!"

Both men had shot and killed one another.

Scared witless, Walter, Howard, and Johnny were hightailing it out of the ditch and back up the tracks before the two men expelled their last breaths. Literally trampling each other in the process, the boys made their way back to Lake Hill as quickly as their legs could carry them. No one dared look back. No one dared slow down. No one uttered a word until they arrived at the front porch of Walter's cabin.

Later, in the safety of Walter's house and frightened beyond anything they'd ever experienced, the boys formed a pact, promising never to utter a word to anyone else about what they'd witnessed that night.

News of the shooting spread throughout the town. Word travels fast, especially after a double killing, even in a town as violent as Middlesboro. What surprised the boys most, however, was the talk in the next few weeks of things happening at the house where the shooting took place. Outlandish stories circulated concerning the gate in the front yard. People told about locking the gate, only to find it unhooked and swinging open on its own a few minutes later. They said when the gate was unlocked, it would swing back and forth, even if no wind was blowing.

Within a few months, no one even wanted to walk the tracks past the house anymore, including Walter, Howard, and Johnny.

The gate wasn't the only thing giving everyone the jitters. Strange activity was happening in the house as well. The lady who lived there—the boys had heard her screaming that night—was telling stories of unexplained noises like footsteps and drips coming from her empty attic. Footsteps out on the porch when no one was there. Loud bangs and falling sounds, as if the shooting was reoccurring. Even though she'd been at the house when the murders happened and was convinced the angry spirit of her dead brother, the man who'd died and fallen back into the house, was the source of much of the strange happenings, she refused to vacate the house.

Every time the boys heard another story about the place, they would just go along with it like everyone else. They dared not mention their unique viewpoint on the subject. The swinging gate mystery from the "Mud Lick Shootout" quickly became a story everyone in the community knew. Rumors and tales surrounding the event died down as time passed. As difficult as it was for our three young witnesses, they kept their promise and never spoke of that night, putting the horrible event behind them.

For a while.

One day Howard approached Walter and Johnny with news none of them expected.

He whispered, "You know the lady livin' in that house where we…seen you know what, is pretty scared still. She's heard things. Seen some things that's got her shook up."

"So what?" Walter said, not very happy to hear the subject brought up.

Howard struggled with how to put it but didn't beat around the bush too long. "Well, come to find out, my daddy's friends with the widow Johnson. He felt bad for her. Daddy's afraid of haints."

"And?" Johnny asked.

"She asked him if he knew of anyone that might could stay with her some nights until the haints or whatever calmed down," Howard said, looking terribly forlorn.

"And?" Walter asked, eyes getting wider.

Howard cleared his throat. "I guess daddy thought I was the one to help her out since I didn't believe much in such things. He's done went and volunteered me. I gotta go stay with her starting next week."

All three of the boys went quiet.

Howard said, "What am I gonna do, fellas?"

Walter stifled a laugh. "We know what you ain't gonna do much of. Sleep."

LARRY D. THACKER *lives in Johnson City, Tennessee, with his wife Karin. His books include four full poetry collections,* Drifting in Awe, Grave Robber Confessional, Feasts of Evasion, *and* Gateless Menagerie, *two chapbooks,* Voice Hunting *and* Memory Train, *and the non-fiction folk history,* Mountain Mysteries: The Mystic Traditions of Appalachia. *His three fiction collections include* Working it Off in Labor County, Labor Days, Labor Nights: More Stories, *and* Everyday, Monsters *(co-written with CM Chapman). He is also a cast member on the Netflix original series Swap Shop.*

— TWENTY-ONE —

WHAT ANNIE SAW
Ashe County, North Carolina

CHRISSIE ANDERSON PETERS

Tragedy befell John Hawkins Hash and his second wife, Elizabeth Hawks Hash, on February 6, 1892, in the small community of Grassy Creek, which is tucked away in Ashe County in the mountains of Western North Carolina. Family legend says they were found huddled together in bed. John was seventy-nine and Elizabeth was fifty, according to their tombstones in the Elijah Anderson Cemetery.

Most records indicate John and Elizabeth had eleven children; some list the number as eight. At least three were of an age where they would still be living at home when their parents died. One was my great-great-grandfather, John

Daniel Hash, who would have been thirteen years old. John Daniel kept mostly to himself as an adult and never talked much about anything, but dressed impeccably and was quite debonair for a man of his means.

I started asking questions about him on an email list shortly after the genealogy bug bit me in 2005. That's how I learned of the horrific way John and Elizabeth died. No one in my family had ever heard the story. John Daniel never told anyone still living (he died in 1955, at age seventy-six). I immediately wondered so many things. Where were he and the other two children? How did they survive when their parents froze to death? Was it a freak snowstorm? Did John and Elizabeth run out of wood? It seemed unlikely for a family in the mountains of Western North Carolina to be that ill-prepared in early February. Were they sick and unable to take care of themselves? Did they have something contagious, and no one would come help them? That also seemed unlikely, given the loyalty of mountain families. I could think of a dozen questions but had no answers.

I even went to the site where John and Elizabeth's home once stood but couldn't make myself get out of my SUV. Something seemed wrong. I could work for days on end in the cemetery in the same community where they were buried, but their property somehow felt off-limits, so I drove away, careful to put the coordinates into my GPS so I could go back if I ever changed my mind.

Still, I wanted answers, and kept searching archives and email lists. I even went to reunions that weren't for my direct-line family to try to learn more. John and Elizabeth lived near his younger sister Sarah and her husband John Hash (a cousin). The day of the reunion included storytelling about Sarah and John and their family and tours of the different ancestral lands up and down the New River in that vicinity.

Another event took people up on the mountain to the family cemetery. For anyone unfamiliar with the region, unless cemeteries are part of established, ongoing church communities, it's common for them to fall into disrepair. Graves are trampled, stones broken by cattle or wild animals, or simply eroded by weather and time. That was not the case with these graves. The family made great efforts to maintain the area, even putting up fencing and dates, replacing headstones when needed, and placing headstones for unidentified persons once identified. They even brought in licensed authorities to make sure things were done correctly when the fencing went up. That's when our cousin Annie's involvement began.

I traveled up that rutted mountainside road in the back of the truck several times that afternoon, drawn to the cemetery in inexplicable ways. I love family cemeteries and always have. Each trip up the hill, Annie's daughter Glenda, who rode as part of the tour, fielded questions about the farm, the cemetery, general family information. And each trip, someone inevitably asked, "Where's your mom, Glenda? Why isn't Annie coming up?" All the reasons boiled down to Annie being tired and wanting to visit with family at the potluck at the cabin site.

On the final trip up to the cemetery for the day, however, when almost no one was left to traverse the mountain, Annie climbed in the back of the truck. I watched her as she looked out over the hillsides, as though she were looking for something. I felt like she had some connection to the land that eluded the rest of us. She must have been coming to these reunions a very long time, I decided.

They had told us on our first trip up the mountain that Sarah's and John's slaves were buried in the back row of the cemetery. I had been taken completely by surprise. In our part of Appalachia, we weren't raised to think slavery was a local issue. But there it was, staring me in the face, in my own family. I had continued thinking about it on each trip up the mountain, wondering what their lives had been like, what their names had been, where they had come from, so many things. I was suddenly aware of Annie standing behind me.

"The fact they were buried in the same cemetery, not some separate place, gives an indication of how they were thought of," she said quietly. "But yes, they were still slaves. It's hard to come to grips with."

It was as though she had read my mind. But surely this must be what most people thought about the situation.

"I'm glad you decided to come up this last trip," I said. "You were part of the group that put the fencing up, right? That's an awesome thing you all did to keep this cemetery safe and preserved for the rest of us to come pay our respects—to all of them," I added. "What was that like? Glenda said you had someone from the state here, since you might have to dig up existing graves to put in proper fence lines?"

She paused for several moments, staring off into space. "I don't like to come here because I see people others don't see. And they tell me things."

She waited for my response. My heart quickened and I nodded. I had experienced the phenomena quite often with my great-grandmother, a Hash, when I was just six years old.

"I understand," I quietly answered.

She smiled and said, "I thought you would." I felt a different kind of kinship with Annie then.

"We went by the old fenceposts and grave lines," she told me as we walked the perimeter of the cemetery together. "For most people, that would have been the end of it. They knew I could see and hear, though. That's why I volunteered to come. It was important to me that we get this right if we were going to do it. And as we started measuring off where the fence would be, one of the slaves came to me, frantic. We were leaving her son outside the safety of the fence. She told me where his grave was. She didn't understand why he wasn't placed in the back with the rest of them, but he was closer to the front, over to the side. And the trajectory of the fence as we had it would leave him outside, away from her." She stopped and pointed to the spot, then started walking in that direction. "I told them they had to stop with the fencing, that there was a problem. And I explained to the state man we needed to dig over here, that there was a body out of bounds. The body would be an eight-to-ten-year-old male child of

African descent. He needed to be placed with his mother. And I told them where the grave needed to be."

Annie stopped at the space where the fence stood now. "It wasn't enough for me that he be inside the fence line. He needed to be with his mother, with his family. He deserved that. And as long as I was involved, he would have that courtesy." When the digging was finished, the state man examined the bones. Her identification of the bones—before ever seeing them—had been correct in race, gender, and age; the spot where they were located was precise. She identified three other similar instances that day, but only went into detail about that one.

"She was lucky you were here," I said, looking at the back row of the cemetery, wondering if the woman was, even now, watching us.

"No," Annie countered, "I was lucky she was here."

As we started walking back toward the pickup for our ride down the hill, she put her hand on my arm. "You're descended from John and Elizabeth. You want to know about their passing, about how they froze to death together?"

My heart lurched. Annie knew details other cousins wouldn't know. "Yes, please, tell me what you know."

"Have you been to their old homeplace?" she asked.

"I have, but I didn't get out. You've been? What did they tell you?"

"They wouldn't tell me, but you're their direct descendant; you might be the one they're waiting to share it with. They might tell you more readily. Their spirits are there, though."

I nodded. Not the answer I hoped for.

"But if you go," she warned me, "be sure to look out for the little boy. He's still very troubled."

"What little boy?"

But the ride down the mountain had ended. The magic of our conversation clicked off as quickly as it had begun. I tried to engage her via email several times, imploring her to tell me more about the little boy. All she would say was that they weren't her line to untangle. And all these years later, despite my questions about what happened, I've never made it back to John and Elizaeth's homeplace—maybe out of fear of what I'd find waiting for me there in the form of answers.

A native of Southwest Virginia, **CHRISSIE ANDERSON PETERS** *now lives in Bristol, Tennessee. Peters holds degrees from Emory & Henry College and the University of Tennessee. Her writing has appeared in* Still: The Journal, Pine Mountain Sand & Gravel, Clinch Mountain Review, Mildred Haun Review, Women of Appalachia Project, *and* 23 Tales: Appalachian Ghost Stories, Legends & Other Mysteries. *Her books include* Dog Days and Dragonflies, Running From Crazy, *and* Blue Ridge Christmas. *She is finishing a collection of memoirs,* Chasing After Rainbows. *She loves travel and anything from the eighties.*

— TWENTY-TWO —

THE HOUSE ON BLUEBIRD DRIVE

Knoxville, Tennessee

ANNA WOOLIVER PHILLIPS

I was going to get married once.

He worked nights—and drank. I thought I loved him, and because of that, I tried to love The House, too.

It did not love me.

It was a normal house. He was a normal man. A ranch-style home, made of brick and board, like a thousand others. A home in Fountain City was nothing to sniff at; the housing crisis and mortgage collapse were real. People were ruined, people I knew. He was a good man. I was a good girl. We would have a happy home. It was a blank slate. They called me lucky.

The House had lovely plaster stucco walls. I would run my hands across the cream surface and marvel that they reflected little to no light. There were enough windows, and sheer drapes, but the entire house was dark. The halls felt like they were hiding something. One end of the house beckoned to the other, but I did not want to enter. I would run from the bedroom to the bathroom as fast as I could scoot, only to envision someone waiting for me on the other side of the closed door.

His ex-wife had painted the bathrooms orange and yellow. Now I know why.

I bought lamps. I left lights on.

It didn't work.

She had battled the darkness there too, hadn't she?

He worked at night and slept in the day. I gradually became his nighttime companion as well. We would drink bottles of wine and watch fireflies in the tops of the trees for hours. It felt magical, if I was drunk and didn't turn around. The windows felt like eyes watching me. I would peer into them, expecting to see someone staring back. Nothing was ever there. I would stand at the oven, with something behind me, and a dark window in front of me. Staring into the night it felt like something was there, just beyond my vision. I would steel my courage and turn around. Nothing.

He worked nights. I needed to sleep at night.

His bedroom was out of the question. When I slept with him, I would have night terrors. Waking up to screams, often unable to tell if they were dreams, or audible. Was it me? Was I screaming? No matter how freshly laundered the bedding was, the sheets always felt greasy. I would lie in the dark with him and feel the heavy coverlet settle.

Then the fingers.

Tiny taps of fingers on the sides of my legs. Up and down. Taps on the mattress that echoed through my bones. I would feign sleep, rigid with terror, waiting for him to awake, as the taps outlined my body.

Frustrated, he suggested I bring my childhood teddy bear for comfort, but even that old friend did not afford me sleep. Up I stayed, to all hours, creeping home to my parent's house to sleep in safety. My mother and my mamaw were troubled. People were meant to sleep at night and wake in the daytime. My dark circles were permanent. I would recite the Lord's Prayer over and over. I begged to sleep on the couch with him in the dark cave of the front room. It felt like a keeping room. Something lived there. I was being haunted.

It spoke to me in June. Exhausted, one night I sat on the couch in the liminal space between coming daylight and the darkest night, 4:30 a.m.

"Hello Anna."

The House whispered in my right ear. It was no man, but neither was it any woman I had ever heard. My hair stood on end up and down my arms. I was climbing the walls in fear. Was I going crazy? It was THE HOUSE.

My aunt, a clairvoyant and spiritualist, felt the spirit of a possessive woman. A woman who wanted him, without me. He scoffed at this. His friends laughed and drank beer, cursing the "ghost." A loud bang echoed through the house with no explanation. They made eye contact in eerie silence. They did not laugh again.

He stopped smiling at me soon after.

He'd given me a ring, a beautiful token, but this talisman was tainted with darkness and doubt. A large black line split the emerald cut diamond I had coveted so. Inclusions add character, don't they?

We had character. We had a haunted house.

I started staying with my parents again while he worked. The ring he gave me started feeling heavy on my hand. It was beyond lovely—exactly what I thought my heart wanted, but it was heavy. So heavy on my hand. I started taking off the ring at night. I would stare at it in the shower, glaring at the inclusions, marveling at the weight. My misery was insurmountable. "This is not my ring" would reverberate through my mind, day and night.

Walking in the house became almost impossible. He changed. He was not the same. He became mean, drank more. I became despondent. We lived like vampires, and the bottles of red wine tasted like blood to me. One day in March when the invitations had been mailed out, and on a day that I wore electric blue for courage and protection, he took back the promises. I freely left the ring.

I left the house and that life, returning to the sun. To normal sleep and wake schedules. It was like waking up. The air was fresh and light again. Was it all in my mind? Was it a tulpa, created from my misery, and by his? I do not care to know. I have never returned and assume that The House still retains its possessive spirits.

I am happy now.

I rarely find a reason to think of him, but sometimes I wonder about The House.

ANNA WOOLIVER PHILLIPS *is a native of Knoxville, Tennessee. Descended from coal miners and gentlemen river boat captains, Anna hails from a large South Knoxville family. A University of Tennessee alumna, she's usually in her urban garden when not moonlighting as a local librarian and small business owner. Momma to a bitty baby, a black cat, and a standard poodle, Anna takes her husband to cemeteries and graveyards around the world and writes non-fiction and fiction inspired by her Appalachian heritage.*

— TWENTY-THREE —

MAY ALL YOUR DREAMS COME TRUE

Knoxville, Tennessee

VICTORIA JORDAN

"May all your dreams come true" was written on the back of the framed photo he gave to her. No signature. Suitably innocuous. No hint as to the true nature of their relationship should someone someday find this photo.

But everybody in the family knew the not-so-mysterious gentleman. Handsome, with sharp symmetrical features. Dapper in a gray fedora, conservative pinstripe suit wearing the wide silk geometric patterned tie typical of the mid-nineteen thirties. He was the love of my great aunt Helene's life. Hank.

The second oldest of my grandmother's nine siblings, born in Milwaukee in 1900, baptized Helen, my great aunt moved to Chicago when she was eighteen and changed her name to Helene. She dropped the "ski" from her last name and assumed a less ethnic, more sophisticated sounding moniker.

Helene trained as a nurse and served as a nanny for wealthy families while working in retail, eventually specializing in women's foundation garments: corsets, brassieres, garter belts, and lingerie. She opened a shop on Chicago's Miracle Mile, not far from Marshall Field's, which became the place women of means went to be fitted for elegant underthings.

My great aunt lived the high life in nineteen-thirties Chicago, selling intimate garments to the wives of wealthy industrialists and mobsters' girlfriends. Her home was a spacious apartment in a white marble skyscraper hotel overlooking Lake Michigan. She claimed she never cooked but lived on room service and dinners at fancy restaurants. During the Depression, she wore a mink coat and carried expensive purses. "You can tell a lot about a woman by her handbag... even if it's empty!" she always said.

Every week a dozen yellow roses arrived from Hank. He also provided her with generous gifts of jewelry, which she wore all at once, along with glittery costume baubles.

The story of where and how they met has been lost to time. Her brothers and sisters have been gone for decades. I don't remember hearing an unkind word about Hank.

My uncles liked the man. Helene's sisters refrained from gossiping. Except to say "Don't get involved with a married man. You'll always be alone on holidays. And you can't even go to his funeral."

A salesman who traveled from Boston to Chicago monthly, Hank left his wife, his four children and his life in New England behind to do his work and live a duplicitous life with my aunt during the second week of each month.

Maybe that's all a man could take. She was not easy to be with.

Helene was demanding, opinionated, obstinate, and psychic. The most unconventional member of an otherwise conventional family.

My aunt could repeat secret conversations back to relatives about events she had no logical way of knowing. Helene told fortunes. She read Tarot cards, tea leaves, and palms. And she wasn't afraid to share bad news. Many family members and friends were brought to tears by her predictions. Helene could be sassy, hysterically funny, and more than a little spooky.

One Christmas in the early nineteen forties, Helene drove her big, green sedan up to Milwaukee to visit relatives for the holidays. Huge parties were always planned. Her sisters' families hosted feasts with several generations filling bungalows and Victorian homes on Milwaukee's South Side.

Young and old family members squeezed into living rooms and parlors dominated by fat Christmas trees strung with bubble lights, bright ornaments, and shiny lead tinsel. Santa arrived on Christmas Eve. Brisket was served after midnight

Mass. Turkey, ham, bountiful side dishes were enjoyed along with stollen, pies and Christmas cookies on Christmas Day and at additional holiday parties in the days that followed. Traditions that continued well into my adulthood.

When it was time for Helene to head back to Chicago, there were some concerns expressed regarding the weather, but no one told Helene what to do. She loaded up her car with gifts and leftovers, fastened her hat, buttoned up her mink coat, pulled short black galoshes over her high heels, and drove off in the late afternoon as it grew dark.

Aunt Helene traveled the two-laned historic Highway 41 several times each year alone. She was familiar with the route. It was only a few hours drive past the vast farms to get back to her home in the big city. She knew where she was going. But maybe there was a detour that night? Maybe the swirling snowflakes hypnotized her? She was snow blind, yet she continued to inch forward.

Tall white drifts obscured her way until she couldn't tell if she was on the road or in a fallow corn field. There were far fewer cars to follow in those days. Helene was lost. She was off the highway. Scared. The sky was dark. The temperature dropped. Snow, still falling, too deep to walk to any of the faintly illuminated farmhouses dotting the fields in the distance.

Just as she began to panic, Hank came to her. Helene recounted the story of that night, how she could feel the warmth of his body. She could hear his heartbeat and his breathing. He was there—in the car—with her.

Hank told her, "Stop the car! I'm here. It's going to be all right."

Helene turned off the big Chevrolet. She reached into the backseat for Christmas gifts of sweaters and a blanket. Nibbled on a cookie, then fell asleep as if in his arms.

She awoke with the sunrise sparkling on the frozen fields. The snow had stopped. Helene blinked and was startled to find she had stopped at the edge of a deep ravine. The car would have dropped into a frozen river had she gone further.

Hank was gone. She could feel he was gone.

My aunt managed to get her hulking vehicle out of the cornfield and back on 41 and the rest of her drive was uneventful.

When Helene arrived at her hotel, there was a telegram waiting for her at the front desk. Hank died. He died the night before at the same time he came to help her. But she already knew that.

She didn't attend his funeral.

Helene never dated anyone after that, though she had suitors. She never married. She eventually moved back to Milwaukee. My aunt continued working well into her seventies and lived an interesting life of parties and travel. In her later years I remember her as the most glamorous woman at the nursing home in her purple tops with her white hair. And always too much jewelry. She lived a full life until she was ninety-five. Content, as if many of her dreams had come true.

When I was twelve, my Aunt Helene gave some books to me: Numerology, Astrology, Theosophy, Eastern Philosophy. Of her twenty or so nieces and nephews, I'm the one she said has "it."

She often took me to lunch at nice restaurants. Most often we ate at Toy's Chinese restaurant, the Pfister Hotel, and Mader's before going to see movies: Tammy, The Sound of Music, Mary Poppins. Aunt Helene encouraged me to be curious about our world, to try new things. I have wonderful memories of interesting conversations about things others don't understand. Aunt Helene taught me there is much we don't know.

Now I'm older than my Aunt Helene was when she told me this story. I look at my hands and they are speckled with the same age spots she had. I have her figure, too. I have Hank's photo, and I have her books. More than once, during a dark time, one of those books fell off my shelf, and opened to just the passage I needed to read to get through to a brighter day. I'm used to weird things happening.

Aunt Helene's predictions of my future were spot on. At least for the first half of my life. She never warned me about divorce or moving so far from family. I never expected to live in East Tennessee. But my fortune didn't predict how happy I would be in my seventies, in my marriage, or the many wonderful friendships I've enjoyed since moving here. It's a beautiful place to live. With its history, ghost stories, and hauntings, I feel right at home.

My sons' lives were enhanced by moving here, too. They both had a great childhood, made many life-long friends, and met their wives at the University of Tennessee. Now I have five healthy, happy grandchildren.

I've been encouraged to share my stories with their kids. In a few years, I'll be passing along Aunt Helene's books because more than one of my grandchildren has "it." That makes me happy. I think Helene would be happy, too. She's still with me. I hear her voice. She's standing behind me as I write this. We've come a long way together from Milwaukee.

All in all, my dreams have come true.

After a career in real estate, retirement provides **VICTORIA JORDAN** *time to use writing skills cultivated at the University of Wisconsin. Jordan also participated in poetry, short story, and screenwriting groups in the Knoxville Writers Guild. She has remained actively involved in East Tennessee's arts and music community while continuing to discover the natural beauty of this area with her husband, Michael. And, just once in a while, she gets a whiff of her great aunt Helene's Estee Lauder perfume to remind her that ghosts do, indeed, exist.*

— TWENTY-FOUR —

I'VE NEVER SEEN JIM MITCHELL

Plainfield, Vermont

STEVEN PAPPAS

To be clear—and honest—I have never seen Jim Mitchell.

I know people who have put eyes on him—and they most definitely should not have: He's been dead a long time now. I have seen things that could be related to Jim Mitchell that I cannot explain. Logic has been lost, along with physics' unwavering laws. That's saying something because I'm pretty cynical. I am a journalist, with years behind me. I trust facts and science.

The idea of Jim Mitchell is cool to me. I suppose I want to believe in ghosts, UFOs, even Sasquatch, but facts—and the concrete, hard reality that comes with them—usually deprive me of such daydreams. Yet I cannot explain what happens on my family's property in rural Vermont, in my corner of a quiet, little town. It is so beautiful here because of Jim Mitchell's life, I can understand not wanting to leave it, even in death. I cannot fathom what that choice must be like, what opportunity he must have missed along the way.

But Jim Mitchell has opted to stay. Or was chosen to stay. Or had to stay.

In some ways, Jim Mitchell is everywhere, all year, and magnificently so. He was a trailblazer in his field, practically a Vermont hero. In the end, though, Jim Mitchell was just a man, destined for legacy and a New Hampshire grave far from where he haunts. By all accounts, he was a very good man. So goes the telling. It spans generations and involves the most random witnesses. Old Jim Mitchell toddles around with the memories of disparate individuals, many more ardent naysayers than I, a few people who knew him, and a slew of eyewitnesses who would probably deny that what they saw was ever present.

Because Jim Mitchell makes no sense.

No one believes it ... until the latch on the kitchen door clunks open, and an old ghost wanders in.

Apple trees are everywhere here.

There are varieties that do not exist anywhere else on the planet. That's not an exaggeration. No two trees are alike.

That was by design.

Jim Mitchell was an arborist. He ran a tree nursery on Gallup Hill and did research for the state of Vermont. I do not know his origin story—how he came to choose that profession or even how he ended up here—but I know that for decades, he grafted trees to come up with hardy varieties that would do well in Vermont's short growing season on the 44th parallel. He ultimately identified many new apples, and his work has been so sought after that the state's Agency of Agriculture has taken samples of the trees in an attempt to fulfill it.

Some trees Jim Mitchell grafted were grown in unique conditions: on rocky crags; others were planted atop hills in constant sunlight and wind; and others were carefully placed along ledges and stone walls in working fields or along roads or wetlands. Those that have survived the decades are being affected by climate change—something Jim Mitchell never had to consider.

When my grandfather bought an adjacent property in 1946, Jim Mitchell confessed that he had been planting trees around the 250 acres at the top of Gallup Hill because the previous owners had not minded. Neither did my grandparents.

Sharing the dirt road meant lots of conversations, including a welcome recommendation that my grandfather plant a windbreak of red pines around the old farmhouse and outbuildings to provide protection from sharp winds ripping across the ridgeline.

I do not know all the details. However, I know Jim Mitchell was a widower. He was left with a daughter, Katherine, whose life was forever wracked by polio. She was Jim Mitchell's pride, his greatest gift. My grandfather claimed Jim Mitchell spent eight hours a day working the nursery and its trees; eight hours a day reading (often aloud to Katherine); and eight hours each night sleeping. Wherever Jim Mitchell went, Katherine went also. And while there was a small legion of "help" for Katherine—my grandmother included—Jim Mitchell's primary focus was on his daughter's comfort and care. He took it very seriously. He refused any other option than what he could arrange or provide.

By all accounts, Jim Mitchell was a small man, at least physically. I am told he was not much more than five feet tall and was thin as a rail. But he was strong, with sinewy, muscular arms. My grandparents reminisced often about his devotion to Katherine, and how he lifted her—so gently and lovingly—in and out of his vehicle and into her wheelchair or to safe ground. It was part of their ritual Sunday mornings when they attended church with my grandparents. Every description I've ever heard noted that Jim Mitchell was blessed with a full head of thick, messy white hair. He was handsome and wore small spectacles that made him seem professorial. Everyone seemed to agree: He was soft-spoken, kind-hearted, generous in time and spirit, and hard-working. Jim Mitchell also was known for wearing a matching green Dickies set—pants and shirt—around the nursery. I am certain he wore other clothes, but they do not matter for this story.

My grandparents were failed farmers.

They wanted to raise laying hens as part of an operation they named Weathervane Farms. Neither came from farming families, and no books could prepare the newly married couple trying to raise a young family for the trials of a long-neglected farm in the Vermont hills. The shortest version of the story is: They got their priorities wrong; they bought too much grain, which turned moldy. The large flock fell ill and had to be dispatched by gassing. The enormous grain bill put them in the hole before they ever really got started.

Jim Mitchell advised them to lease the land to area farmers and try something else that would keep an income coming in. They did just that. Then three other notable things happened: My grandmother, an English major from Middlebury College, started writing and publishing poetry; my grandfather started jogging; and a golf course expanded "up the road" on a property adjacent to my family's.

That meant my grandmother started documenting her natural surroundings; my grandfather was out on that dirt road a lot; and there was a marked spike in vehicle traffic.

With each season, the apple trees punctuated the way along that stretch of back road, from Jim Mitchell's nursery to the golf course. Through pruning and upkeep, the scraggly trees reached out in a full canopy relatively close to the ground. In winter, the trees were picturesque in their starkness against wide fields of snow; in spring, the trees exploded in sweet blossoms; in summer, the canopy filled in with lush, green leaves and small fruits that, come autumn, came to complete the trees' potential. Some of the apples were red; others were pear-yellow or more greenish. It was a lovely experiment.

In her journals, my grandmother wrote about the orchard and apple trees, or the wildlife that loved them as much as she did. The trees often served as characters featured in some of her more earthy poems. My grandfather measured Vermont's seasons by the trees' progression as he jogged every morning by the orchard, or the random sentinels at a roadside stone wall. The golfers, many of them business owners from around town, envied the quintessential scene atop Gallup Hill.

My grandfather called it "God's country." In fact, it was Jim Mitchell's. And it still is.

Apparently, my grandmother took the call.

Within moments of hanging up, both of my grandparents were in a vehicle and down the hill, pulling into Jim Mitchell's dooryard. When they got inside the house, father and daughter were splayed on the floor. The fall had shattered the old man's arm at the elbow.

It would be the last time Jim Mitchell ever had to carry Katherine.

It was not long—perhaps a year or so from that day but no one can recount for certain—that Jim Mitchell passed. He died at home. Perhaps it was a broken heart or certain guilt over not being able to care for Katherine; or the loneliness of a shattered routine without her; or perhaps it was his age. Records indicate he was eighty-two when he died.

I never learned where Katherine ended up—a missing detail that may be the very reason Jim Mitchell can't seem to leave the place that meant so much to him.

Maybe he stays as penance.

My grandfather served in the U.S. Army. It was ingrained in him to treat officers and his elders with respect. He raised his children and grandchildren to do the same. Whenever he talked about "Mr. Mitchell," it was thus. Never "Jim." I never heard him refer to anyone else with the title.

My role in this tale is in the telling, really. I came along almost a decade after Mr. Mitchell died. As a boy, I knew a different family who lived in "the Mitchell place." They were not Mitchells.

Over time, the unmaintained apple trees got tall and unwieldy. My friends and I played in them across all seasons. For sure, the fruit got more puny by the year. The wildlife still flocked to our corner of town to feast through autumn and early winter, producing fat deer. The stretch of road became known for large herds, which also attracted small gatherings of poachers and other miscreants.

Growing up, I heard stories about Mr. Mitchell—mostly in the context of those trees and the unconditional love he had for his daughter. To me, nothing seemed as potentially good in life as Mr. Mitchell. He was a role model I never knew.

Shortly after my grandmother died when I was ten, I overheard my grandfather mention that he had "seen" his dead wife while out on a morning run. That thought terrified me, and I told him so. He replied, "Don't worry, she's probably just out trying to find Mr. Mitchell."

With that remark, the heavy tumblers clunked into place, and the large door of the story opened: All the years of growing up on the property, I had overheard references—from neighbors, passersby and even strangers—that they had seen a man walking our property, often around the orchard. He always was described as short, white-haired, wearing a green shirt and pants.

We had always given friends and a few neighbors the necessary permission to hunt deer or turkey. The local historical society often had crews doing work on a couple of "sites" that had been among the "original pitches" in our town. The Smith family, who lived even farther up the road, kept up our fields with feed crops for their milking cows. I was used to people—not always family—being on the land with us.

Until that moment, it never dawned on me that one of the people out there might be a ghost.

Most commonly, the concern—often from golfers on their way to or from the course—has been that an "old person" was wandering around in the fields.

Mr. Mitchell has been seen sitting by the orchard. He has been seen at the edge of the road, or down by the pond. A few times, he was spotted walking toward our house or barn, as if intent on delivering a message or getting a tool.

My grandfather insisted folks had stopped by with their query, indicating they had talked to the old man. One neighbor swore that many years ago he, too, had been surprised when seeing his old neighbor over by the Swift farm, a stone's throw from our place. The story goes that they exchanged waves but no words.

As far as we know, there are no connections between the years of witnesses. The story is one we have kept as family lore, except for a few friends or partners who came into the fray.

In some ways, it was hard not to believe in Jim Mitchell. By "being around," he felt like he was part of our extended family.

So let's move this story indoors.

At our kitchen table, one chair put your back to the door and was a little too close to the wood stove. It was rarely used. We jokingly referred to it as "Mr. Mitchell's seat," like the empty chair of a seder.

At one point in time, what was a kitchen in my day had once been an attached shed or outhouse, part of a conversion into a never-completed mother-in-law apartment. Galley style, with an undersized, apartment stove, there could never be too many cooks in that kitchen, but it was a spot for mingling. The space also housed a mustard yellow Maytag washing machine and a top-loading wood stove, as well as the bulky accompanying wood box. What was even more unusual was the room had five doors. One of those doors fed into a small hallway that led to a tiny bedroom and an exterior door on the north side of the house.

While it is a very old house, built in the 1830s, it is sound in construction. By today's standards, nothing is level or plumb. But it was thoughtfully built.

All my adolescent life, the old, wooden door that went to "the north door" was often closed. It took a fair amount of effort to push down on the spoon-shaped thumb latch that lifted a metal bar on the other side of the door that was held in place by a metal lip. The sound of that old latch opening was distinctive because of the effort it took to release it. It was obvious when someone was coming or going.

Growing up, it was not unusual for that thumb latch to click, and that old door would glide open, silent until it bumped the door stopper installed to keep it from striking the wall with a small ringing crash.

"Mr. Mitchell must be visiting," was the running joke.

It did not matter if it was sunny or rainy, windy or still, hot or cold, humid or dry: That closed door seemed to prefer to be open. It became a bit of a party trick to close the door and mill around while a meal was being prepared. As if on cue, the latch would go, the door would open, and everyone would turn to look into the dark hallway. It freaked out more than a few guests.

Sometimes, too, when you were in one end of the farmhouse, you could hear people talking at the other end. But if you investigated, no one was ever there. Also, with windows and doors closed, you would occasionally hear a door, drawer, or cabinet close somewhere. And the floors creaked with the weight of mystery.

All old house stuff.

In the autumn of 2007, my grandfather passed away in that house, on a hospital bed in a front room, just to add to the mystique of another possible haunting.

In the weeks following, I needed to remove some large furniture from the old farmhouse. A work colleague—a fellow journalist—had a metal track for sliding large objects (think conveyor belt). One afternoon, we were guiding a large metal desk through the cluttered dining room and into the kitchen. Hopefully, we would be able to turn it forty-five degrees in the kitchen space and then guide the monstrosity out on the porch and dump it onto the lawn, where it could be dealt with later.

My friend was amazed and a bit disgusted by the stacks and piles of clutter and the general filth of the old house. My grandfather had been hoarding in his final years, so there was a lot of a lot. We struggled to get the desk up on one end, and we were easing it through the dining room doorway; he was in the kitchen, and I was on the other side. I heard him say, "You looking for Steve? Hold on."

"Steve, someone's here to see you," he called from the other side of the desk.

We could not just drop it. We carefully eased it down and got the desk to a point where it would not tip over or crush things. I had to walk around, through another part of the house, to get to the kitchen.

When I walked into the space, my friend pointed to the open door in the kitchen. "He went in there," he said.

That door.

I could see the hallway was dark. To combat winter's chills, my grandfather had closed off the north entrance with crude framing and layers of thick, clear plastic.

No lights were on.

"Hello?" I called out. I walked into the hallway, opening the door to the back bedroom, which was also dark and cluttered. It smelled musty. No one was there, and there was no way to get out other than through the doorway in which I was standing.

I walked back into the kitchen and said, "Where'd they go? Who was it?"

Surprised and confused, my friend said, "I don't know. It was an old man."

"Short, white hair, wearing green Dickies?" I asked, nodding before I got an answer.

"Yeah," he said.

"Bill, you lucky bastard," I said. "You just saw a ghost."

A family of farmers live in that house today.

I built a smaller, more efficient home just up the road, still within sight of the farmhouse's roof, as well as the orchard across the road. My new home incorporates some of the red pines and cherry trees my grandfather planted at Jim Mitchell's urging all those years ago to keep out those wicked winds. There are always apple trees around us.

That young family—loving parents and two little ones—heard my stories about Jim Mitchell and even saw the kitchen door party trick long before they ever moved in. They were neighbors and friends first. The door still does its thing, and while they have not seen Jim Mitchell, there have been hints of little hauntings both inside the house and out in the fields, including some inexplicable voices overheard by the farm hands. Like me, they are not scared of what can't be explained. In fact, they seem grateful of the mystery held inside that windbreak—all of us a big family of living and dead.

STEVEN PAPPAS *is a journalist living in Vermont on land that has been in his family for generations. He has worked in newsrooms around the Northeast, as both a reporter and an editor.*

COMING SOON

OPEN HOUSE

Mostly True Tales of Crazy in Southern Real Estate

SUZY TROTTA

HOWLING HILLS PUBLISHING

OPEN HOUSE:
TRUE TALES OF CRAZY IN SOUTHERN REAL ESTATE

Think you know about real estate?

Forget everything you've seen on TV and get a real behind-the-scenes tour as one Southern agent navigates a career helping people buy and sell homes.

Suzy Trotta deals with things real estate school never taught her, from pet roosters to stalkers to her own willingness to do almost anything for a sale. The author exposes a side of the industry most people never hear about, and she does it in candid detail.

This open house is sometimes funny, rarely glamorous, and always entertaining. You may never look at home buying the same again.

AVAILABLE NOW

23 tales

APPALACHIAN GHOST STORIES, LEGENDS & OTHER MYSTERIES

EDITED BY
TERRY SHAW & BRAD LIFFORD

HOWLING HILLS PUBLISHING

23 TALES:
APPALACHIAN GHOST STORIES, LEGENDS & OTHER MYSTERIES

The words by twenty-three writers are captured in a mix of ghost stories and paranormal experiences, mysteries from history that persist to this day, and weird beings that haunt the backwoods and pierce the night with mournful wails. These stories—from Georgia to Virginia and Pennsylvania, from Kentucky to Tennessee and West Virginia—will raise the hair on your neck, touch you, and even make you laugh.

The writers of 23 Tales had just one main charge from Howling Hills: The stories could not be fiction. So, pull up a chair. What these writers are about to tell you is true.

AVAILABLE NOW

East Tennessee
GARDEN STORIES

Sharing Knowledge, Celebrating Heritage, and Building Community

EAST TENNESSEE GARDEN STORIES: SHARING KNOWLEDGE, CELEBRATING HERITAGE, AND BUILDING COMMUNITY

East Tennessee Garden stories is about people, their love of gardening, and what we can learn from them. This beautifully designed, large format book (8.5x11) includes 150 vivid color photos and tips on things like ditching your lawn for a garden, building soil, turning discarded windows into a greenhouse, and more. Most of all, it's like visiting with friends who like to swap garden stories.

www.ingramcontent.com/pod-product-compliance
Lightning Source LLC
Chambersburg PA
CBHW070626030426
42337CB00020B/3934